CM0074155G

VIVIENNE WESTWOOD SHOES

edited by
Luca Beatrice and Matteo Guarnaccia

DAMIANI

Luca Beatrice

In the history of contemporary art there's a profound difference, which perhaps cannot be explained only by the generation gap, between artists who emerged before and after 1975. The mid 70's are in fact the real watershed between a chiefly ethical conception – the need to change the world was something that regarded art and artist – and its opposite in which art was once more seen as a wholly aesthetic object with no other task than to be consumed within itself. The artists who reached their peak between slightly pre-'68 and around '75 maintained in their work a commitment to changing the world, whereas those who emerged in the late 70's accepted the system as it was, devoting themselves to more interiorised reflections. The beautiful came once more to prevail over the useful, though only in a broad sense. So in the first case art walked with ideology, philosophy, politics and society, whereas in the second case reflection took place on the plane of taste, of the relationship with divertissement, seeking to discover (or rediscover) shadow zones formerly confined to a narrow cultural context but at last coming to the forefront.

Vivienne Westwood shares (with few other artists and creative people) a very special age-time condition: when she debuted and made her name in the world of visual culture the definitive mutation that dissolved the tensions of the ethical into the playful had not yet occurred. It was no longer the 70's and not yet the 80's. In this sense fashion, still not completely considered art inasmuch as the process of deliverance from ideological fences was at an early stage, became a privileged storehouse of ideas, images and solutions. Fashion understood as triumph of inspiration, genius, creative talent, and far from transforming itself into an autonomous system. Attention in fact focused on rare excellences and not on a generalised economy. Success came only to those who managed to imbue their creations not only with forms but also sociologically relevant content, as had happened in the 60's with Mary Quant's miniskirt. Westwood intuited the power of a mix between street style (aided by the cut'n'up techniques with which punk was coming forward and which finally made it possible to match things of different origin, freeing them from the weight of their intrinsic meaning) and high culture, including references to the history of art. In fact it wasn't just by chance that the so-called punk period fed, and how, on those subversions and splits that posited it as the last avant-garde of the 20th century. But at the same time we can't help noticing the references to tradition and the past which already in some way opened onto the post-modern era. *The Great Rock'n'Roll Swindle,* Julian Temple's film about the Sex Pistols (1979), begins with a scene in period costume, full of crinolines, lace and pirate style, a homage to Francis Drake, ambivalent hero of the

Elizabethan age. Derek Jarman's *Jubilee* (1978) tells a punk story also set in the past, where the seditious matrix is intended as the thread running through different epochs. An image to keep duly in mind as soon as we mention the *Seditionary Boots,* invented by Vivienne Westwood quite simultaneously with Jarman's film, for the 1976 collection. As if to say that the wearer of these highly unusual boots automatically stands outside the law and is against any kind of system then and now, if only by means of an aesthetic sign. Not to mention that the most immediate reference, often recognised among the historical roots of punk, is Situationism, which is to say a movement of subversive ideas which did not aspire to formalisation in an enclosed work of art but rather to leaving behind traces, clues, fragments and above all red herrings.

A similar reflection, fundamental to Vivienne Westwood and the artists of her generation, concerns profound change, also datable to around 1975, in the use of the human body as a vehicle for sensations, emotions and ideas, both within the work of art and in its social fallout. If the "traditional" Body Art of the late 60's and early 70's had exhausted its leading role, sliding from subversion into inevitable repetition and mannerism, a new frontier was being crossed and the body was able to take on new values and tensions, for example an explicit sexuality, provocative but not politicised.

Those were the days of the new underground in New York (names like Nick Zedd, Lydia Lunch and Richard Kern were the leading figures of a new iconography of the body by means of anti-conventional, de-structured clothes that formalised a street style, gloomy but with great attention paid to the slightest detail). More than anything they were signs designed for individual use and not for the collective identification of a group.

These and other stylistic and cultural motifs form an integral part of Westwood's more than thirty year itinerary, both in the invention of clothes and in the very special and rich footwear sector where her creative genius is exalted, reaching peaks of exceptional inventiveness. A determining factor in Westwood's poetics is complete refutation of the evolutionistic system (where one thing naturally succeeds another and is put forward as its progressive development) in favour of continual recourse to a figurative treasure where insights return, are reprised and re-formalised and, above all, take on value when they are made to act in a new and different context.

Among the hundreds of models Westwood has designed and produced in more than thirty years of collections – all created by blending the craftswoman's care with a style that grasps ferments, overturns archetypes and plays with space-time contradictions in a sort of metaphysical theatre of the absurd – some have left their indelible mark in the contemporary collective imagination. More than anything else with those "prototypes" where the degree of invention is at its peak, hypertrophic to the point of challenging the rules of "wearability", with vertiginous heels or improbable fastenings. The shoe is therefore comparable to a sculpture or a design object, like the celebrated *Buffalo Bag Boot* and its "twin" *Sock Boot*, both produced in 1982, and the historic *Super Elevated* series, cross and delight of the 1993 fashion catwalks with the record 21 centimetre heels. Personally I find the *Super Elevated Cowboy Boot* version irresistible (*Café Society* collection, 1994) with its references to early 70's Glam Rock, its magic and sequins, reprising the look of the New York Dolls, a band that many consider absolutely pre-punk. Continuing in this category we must mention at least models like the *Rocking Horse Boot* (1988) – where there is an ingenious contradiction between Japoniste type sole and heel and the instep in the more canonical leather – and the very precious *Swarowski Sandals* (1998) in leather and plastic.

Right from the start Vivienne Westwood's style has been charged with strong links to the body, in the direction of that post-performance referred to above: we're in the context of an outrageous but elegant sexuality, private and not public, which rehabilitates the taste for voyeurism and tactility in an erotic strategy that envisages not fixed but interchangeable roles, which plays on the casuistry and bizarreness of S/M, Fetishism, Bondage and Leather. In this sense the *Goat Chain Boots* for the 1973-74 *Sex* collection became an absolute must, a cult object comparable only to certain examples of contemporary design, an archetypal boot that Westwood herself has shown off on many occasions. The *Rope Sandals* (*Punkature* collection, 1983) already went beyond the extremisms of punk and introduced – still in a powerfully sexual context – colours like violet (the string laces) and white (the rubber soles). The model I find most exciting, quite aside from clichés, is the *Lace Up Nurse Spoons* (*Erotic Zones* collection, 1995): in effect, a pair of shoes in the governess or nurse style but with a 15.5 centimetre heel, valid also in the versions *Mary Jane Spoons* and *2 Tone Court*, highly elegant in their regimental bicolour. The fetish element, almost a self-reference to the *Sex* epoch, returned with the recent *Bondage Sandals* (2004), while the *Penis Shoes* (1995) obviously need no further comment.

Onto this subversive and ultramodern attitude Vivienne Westwood superimposes another more meditated and cultured one which to date represents the poetics prevalent in her shoe production. In a great number of models, subtle but evident references to art history can be traced (in forms, images and materials) which amplify the English designer's ambition to relate more than ever to the concept of the classical, from the renaissance to the 18th century, from Victorianism to early modernism. The *Pirate Boot*, a model produced in numerous versions from the early 80's to the present, was literally the relay baton passed on from punk to the new romantics, from reinvention of the look to the rise of the new British music scene (Culture Club, Spandau Ballet, Adam and the Ants, the shooting stars Classic Nouveaux, the early Depeche Mode). Westwood particularly loves references to the second half of the 18th century, an age in which figurative art seemed to be awaiting a great social transformation – which punctually arrived with the French Revolution in 1789 – and in the meantime was admiring itself in hyper-decorations charged with nostalgia and an indecipherable feeling of melancholy. (Extraordinary in this sense is the interpretation put forward by Jean Starobinski in his essay *The Invention of Liberty*.) The Westwood collection *Voyage to Cythere* cites, right from the title, one of the most enigmatic works in the history of art, Antoine Watteau's canvas of the same name, intuiting that precisely in a period less oppressive from the point of view of content (as rococo was), creativity appears to be freed from the subject and can focus on unpredictable and surprising forms. These are the moments when inspirations are innumerable and the solutions never taken for granted, when decoration triumphs over meaning: precisely the late 18th century (*Red Boot with Mirror Buckles,* 1989); Flemish painting (*Toile Print Boot,* 1996, painted like Delft pottery – a curious reference could be made to the work of Belgian conceptualist Wim Delvoye); French classicism (*Satyr d'Orsay Pump,* 1995); Oscar Wilde's dandyism in the Victorian era (*Trompe l'oeil Boot Man,* 1996); the Jazz Age as portrayed by Scott Fitzgerald (*Le Flou Faille* collection, 2003), right down to the ironic revisiting of British colonialism (*Sahara Boot,* 1999).

In all this hypertrophic proliferation of forms and images that "walk" in the past as in the present, the ethical intent that animated the first steps taken by Vivienne Westwood's shoes in far off 1973 has certainly not been extinguished. If the *Seditionaries* and the *Pirates* embodied the English designer's outsider orientation, her intention to raise to the peak of the values scale figures which, being mythical, were self-excluded from the social sphere, it is precisely today that Westwood has returned to manifest her explicit dissent. The new collection of shoes and clothes showcases the first-time brand *AR,* meaning *Active Resistance (to Propaganda)* against the politics of the Bush and Blair administrations, and preoccupation about authoritarian changes that threaten civil rights.

MARIE ANTOINETTE'S CROISSANT DIPPED IN MARAT'S BATHTUB

Matteo Guarnaccia

The hazardous double-barrelled term foot-footwear, garden of refined delights (and equally refined agonies), a favoured battlefield of the inexhaustible state of belligerence between physicality and technology, has fascinated, challenged and obfuscated the creativity (and the reason) of illustrious artists and intellectuals, offering limitless stimuli for comment and symbolic-poetic representation. The artistic approach to the subject in modernity is stably governed by three fundamental iconographic coordinates. The two ends of the interpretive spectrum are marked by a materic, chthonic model (work, privation, suffering and empathic transformation) and by an artificial aerial model (indolence, lightness, detachment and indifference) while centre field is occupied by the visionary, liquid gaseous model (magical realism, Pataphysics, playfulness).

The first typology is exemplified by the considerable series of shoes created by Vincent Van Gogh between 1886 and 1887. Heavy, organic objects, like clods of muddy earth, portrayed in the imminence of dissolution, a sequence of "sinister" and odd shoes, social and Brechtian, the fulcrum of heated investigations from Heidegger to Derrida. Part of the same family are the gastronomically appetizing shoes that act with Charlie Chaplin in *The Gold Rush* (1925). The second model includes the icy, funereal domain of Andy Warhol's fetishistic shows (*Diamond Dust Shoes*, 1980); the poetic erotic-space engineering of Britain's John Willie (*Bizarre*, 1946-1959) and Allen Jones (*Night and Day*, 1976) and the divine enveloping ribbons of Yves Saint Laurent. Exactly equidistant from the two models mentioned above lies the freezing Melusina-like uncertainty of René Magritte's mutant object (*Le Modéle Rouge*, 1935) which perfectly seizes the monstrous symbolic indeterminacy of the shoe. Vivienne Westwood's work has every right to step into this Wunderkammer of podalic gems. At ease in the territory of fiction, of the fraud perpetrated against physicality in the name of beauty, she ruminates on ideas between Jones and Magritte (with some ventures into the Leprechauns' workshop, the slippers preferred by fairies). This English artist, with the steady hand of a practised cutthroat, collection after collection implements the fatwa issued by the prophet of aesthetic fundamentalism Oscar Wilde who admonished that "the first duty of man is to be artificial".

Shoes play an essential role in Madame Westwood's arsenal. She understood long ago that the game is not, of course, to offer a suitable solution to the ambulatory needs of a biped mammal but rather to radically increase the coefficient of artificiality and dissimulation, distancing herself disdainfully from the limitations of human anatomy. Hostile to all forms of realism, aristocratically planted on the heights of her towering heels, she has had the healthy courage to affirm without scruples the privilege of an autonomous artist, perfectly capable of defending herself from the vulgarity of the market, from the totalitarian power of the false, and from the levelling that is mercilessly implemented by universal reification. If revolutionaries are suspicious of the beautiful inasmuch as it is a sign of privilege, she vindicates the revolutionary power of privilege and the beautiful. She must be acknowledged for the great achievement of saving the *risqué* shoe from the trap of the closed system of fetishism and for having demystified street culture by rejecting the mystique of trainers, an unknowing apologia for crude behavioural reductionism.

Theatre, the representation that replaces naturalist dogma and the rhetoric of functionalism, is an integral part of the initial and original Westwoodian project, first with her ironic-sentimental reinterpretation of the American Fifties and of sex shop paraphernalia, and subsequently with the happy invention of punk. Signs of a fierce reaction to two decades of wild/unisex utopias – existentialist, beatnik, hippie – distinguished by back-to-nature barefoot, Indian moccasins, Hindustan chopatz, flip-flops, wooden clogs, desire-killing Birkenstocks. Putting a brake on the

barbaric anachronism of the natural foot. Creative maturity arrived with a formal and ideal embracing of Rococo, the great European school dedicated to rendering spectacular the "superfluous", the visionary fantastical, a roguish gallantry. A movement that shared with punk only an absolute laicality and anti-naturalistic disdain ("Nature," said the good Boucher, "is too green and poorly lit"). Westwood's footwear exploded like Marie Antoinette's croissant dipped in Marat's bathtub. It is a post-modern interpretation of the flying object shoe, alluring and concupiscent, which mischievously detaches itself from the foot of the young lady on the swing in *Les hazards heureux de l'escarpolette* (1767) by Jean- Honoré Fragonard.

Westwood offers the woman-courtesan, mistress of herself, splendid pedestals (and boards and stages) to obtain honours, strategic visibility and bold postures. Like the unguent spread on the feet of heroes by the serpent queen in *The Arabian Nights* to make them walk on water, the Westwood stage intervenes on the lower parts of the body with the magic of transformation. Footwear that from being a simple support and aid to movement becomes figurative metaphors. Shoes that are as opulent and intoxicating as a love potion, tooled-up to recall the equestrian roots of western nobility. The morphology of her most famous model, the *Super Elevated Gillie* (1993-1994) a bewitched grafting, a hybrid equine-goat style suited to the frequenters of François Boucher's *Arcadia Felix,* promises and gives heroic climbers the sublime experience of skimming the most amoral precipices of frivolity. An element of criminal craftsmanship, so impudently classic and erudite, worthy of figuring in *Anatomie de l'Image* published by Hans Ballmer in 1957. A perfect idea for bringing down the wall separating woman from her image. An engineering device or sublime fetishistic machine, an elegant and perverse challenge to the force of gravity, to inclined plane physics, that ignores, conceals or even better incorporates, absorbs and perfects the physiological element. Dramatic stilt platforms, elegies to conceptual integrity and to elitism, magnificently ungovernable (model Naomi Campbell's fall has become history) unless you're a giraffe Dogon dancer. The sacrifice is well repaid, and even Samuel Beckett underwent the extreme discomfort of tight shoes in order to imitate the podalic dandyism of his adored master James Joyce. Vivienne Westwood's production should always and in any case be observed with amused preoccupation. Even her innocuous cherry red *Rocking Horse* shoes could turn out to be lethal (flash of genius or flash of blade?) like the realistically socialist footwear worn by Lotte Lenya – Kurt Weill's muse and companion – in her unforgettable caricature performance as the lesbian spy Rosa Klebb of S.P.E.C.T.R.E. in the

James Bond film *From Russia with Love.*

The exhibition that Vigevano has dedicated to Westwood's footwear could be an excellent occasion for the director Manoel de Oliveira – in the event of a less crepuscular version of *Vou para casa* (2001) – to take note of dialogues between shoes, dialogues far more brilliant than the ones described in his film. Imagine the variety of subjects that would arise from conversation at close quarters (only a flight of stairs separates the Stables from the Footwear Museum) between the princely slipper of Beatrice d'Este and the noble rank of London shoes. A dialogue in no way out of place: duchess Beatrice d'Este – "mistress of the house" at Vigevano Castle which is hosting this tribute to the ingenious designer – would be a perfect testimonial for the latter's creations. A marvellous prototype of renaissance woman, full of grace and guts, cultured and beautiful, lover of art and music, of splendour and celebration, who died very young (*too fast to live too young to die*).

Vivienne Westwood's Personal "Goat" Chain Boot

Sex
1973/74

Seditionary Boot

Seditionaries
1976

Hammerhead Trainer

Pirate
A/W 1981

Silver Hammerhead Boot

Savage
S/S 1982

Brocade Hammerhead Ankle Boot

Savage
S/S 1982

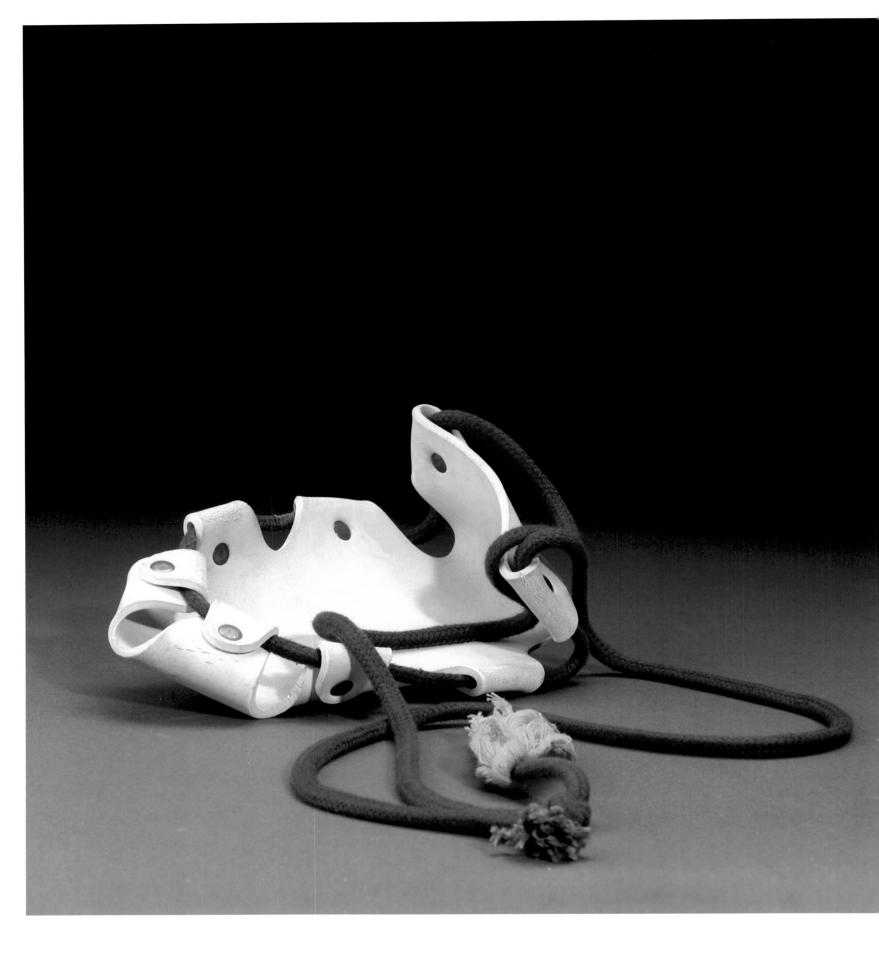

Rope Sandal

Punkature
S/S 1983

Rope Thong Sandals

Hypnos
S/S 1984

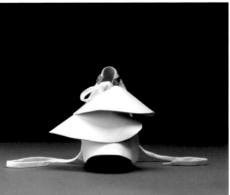

Witches Three Tongue Shoe

Witches
A/W 1983

Three Tongue Trainer

Witches
A/W 1983

Strobe Shoe

Clint Eastwood
A/W 1984

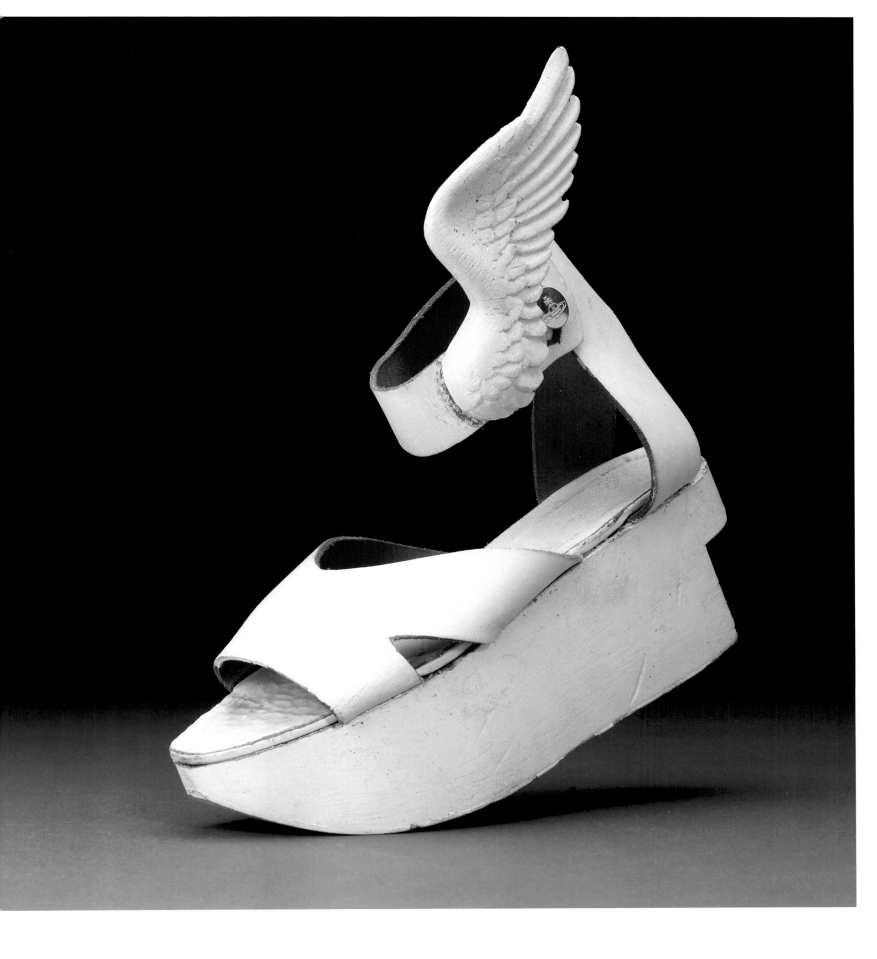

Apollo Wing Shoe

Pagan I
S/S 1988

Patent Mule

Pagan I
S/S 1988

White Boot with Mirror Eyelets

Voyage to Cythera
A/W 1989

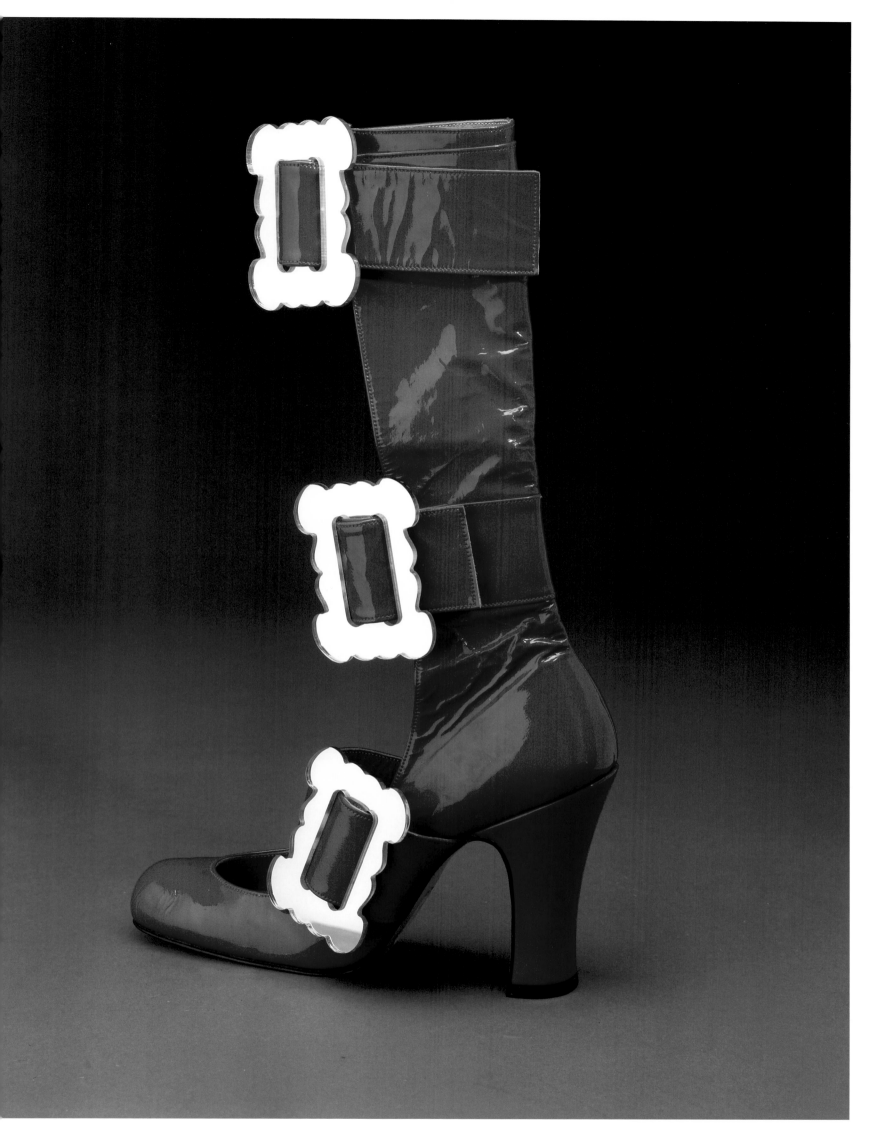

Red Boot with Mirror Buckles

Voyage to Cythera
A/W 1989

Pirate Boot

Pirate
A/W 1981

Pirate Slingback

Man
S/S 2002

Pirate Ankle Boot

Man
S/S 2002

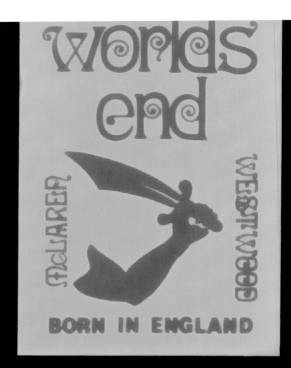

BORN IN ENGLAND

Vivienne Westwood
& Malcolm McLaren
invite

to the
**Worlds End Collection
Autumn - Winter 81 Show**
at the Pillar Hall Olympia
12.30 for 1.00pm
Tuesday 31st March

R.S.V.P.
Marysia Woroniecka

Three Strap Sandal

Savage
S/S 1982

Canvas Three Strap

Man
S/S 2002

Buffalo Sack Boot

Buffalo
A/W 1982

Buffalo Bag Boot

Buffalo
A/W 1982

Anglophilia Sack Boot

Anglophilia
A/W 2002

Anglophilia Bag Boot

Anglophilia
A/W 2002

Elevated Court

Portrait
A/W 1990

Elevated Tartan Lace-Up

Anglomania
A/W 1993

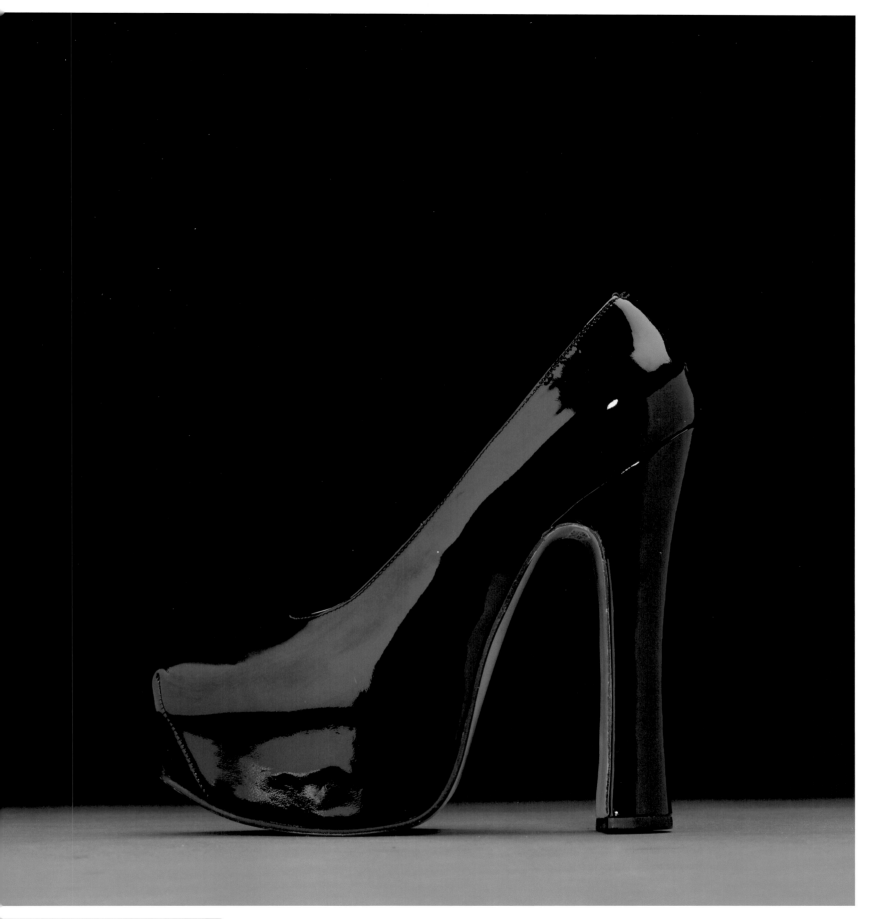

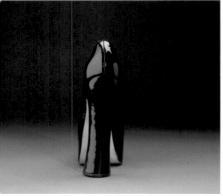

Elevated Court

Portrait
A/W 1990

p 46

Super Elevated Fur Boot

On Liberty
A/W 1994

Elevated Wing Shoe

Portrait
A/W 1990

p 48

Elevated Leopard Boot

Portrait
A/W 1990

Rocking horse ankle boot

Pagan I
S/S 1988

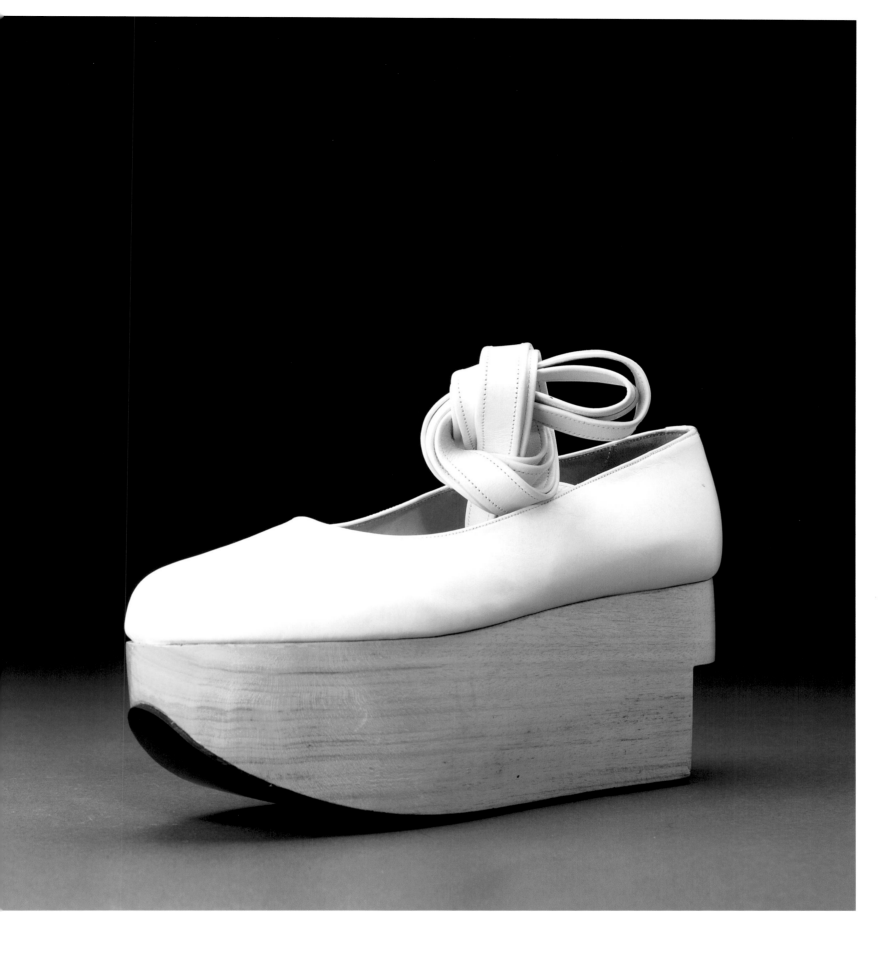

Rocking Horse Ballerina

Harris Tweed
A/W 1986

Rocking Horse Golf Shoe

Time Machine
A/W 1988

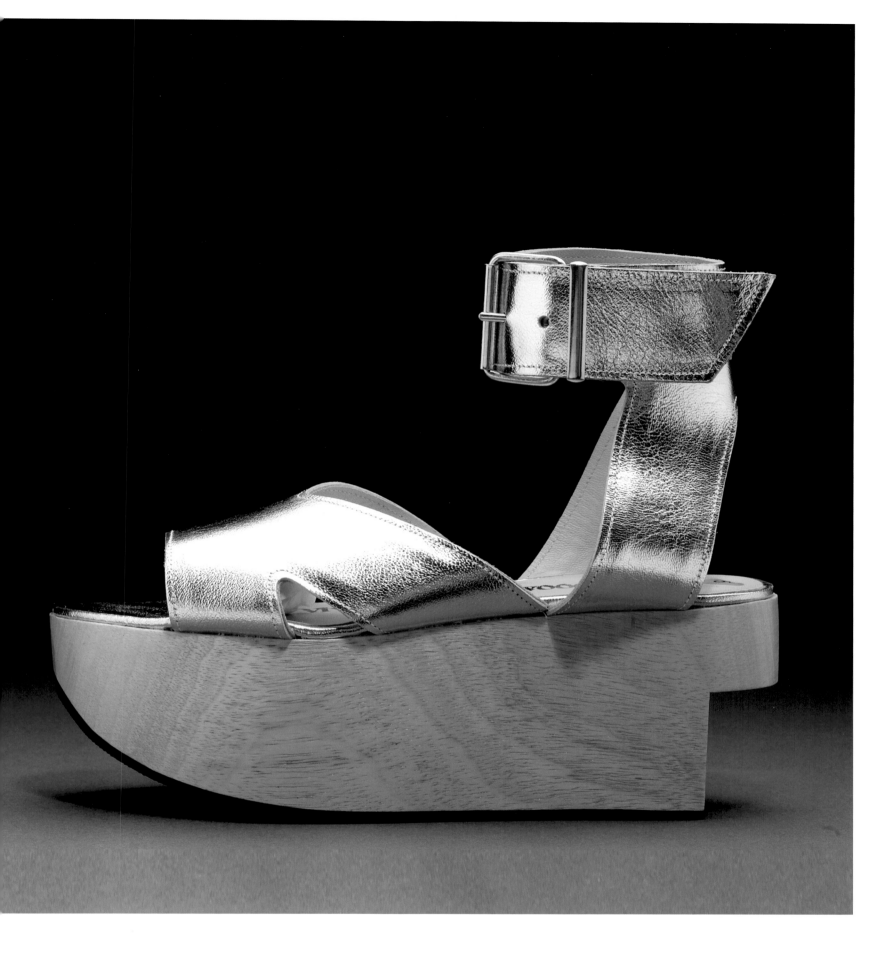

Rocking Horse Slave Sandal

Pagan V
S/S 1990

p.54

Super Elevated Lace-Up Ankle Boot

Grand Hotel
S/S 1993

Mock-Croc Super Elevated Court Shoe

Grand Hotel
S/S 1993

Mock-Croc Super Elevated Gillie

Anglomania
A/W 1993

Cork Wedge

Cafè Society
S/S 1994

Beach Sandal on Cork Wedge

Cafè Society
S/S 1994

Candystripe Fabric Tie Sandal

Cafè Society
S/S 1994

p 62

Super Elevated Cowboy Boot

Cafè Society
S/S 1994

Raffia Mule

Cafè Society
S/S 1994

p 65

On Liberty Riding Boot

On Liberty
A/W 1994

p 66

Spanish Boot

On Liberty
A/W 1994

On Liberty C17th Shoe

On Liberty
A/W 1994

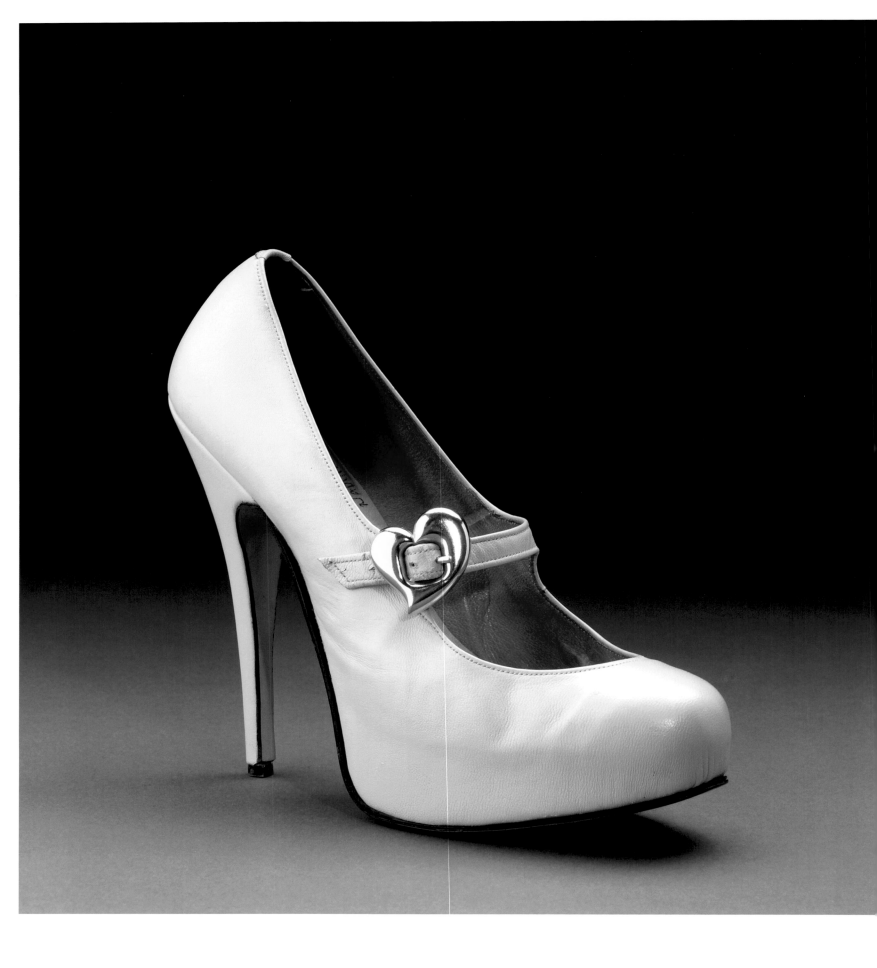

Mary Jane with Heart Buckle

On Liberty
A/W 1994

Lace Up Nurse Spoon

Erotic Zones
S/S 1995

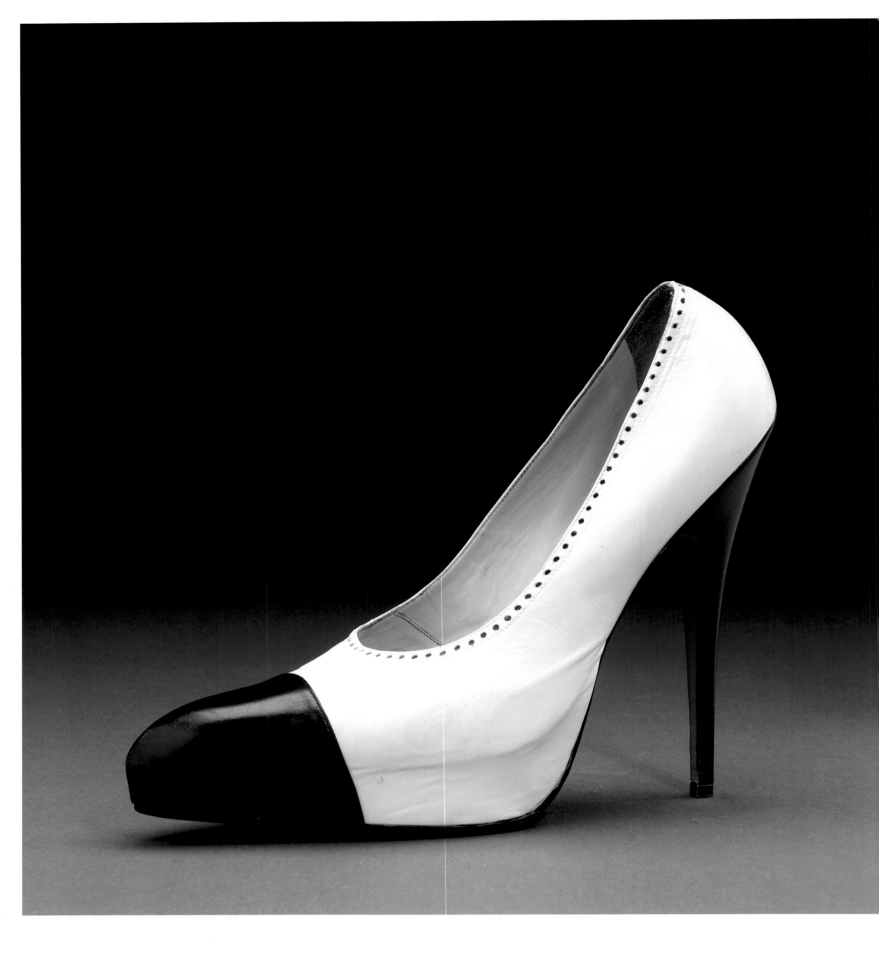

Two-Tone Court

Erotic Zones
S/S 1995

Penis Shoe

Erotic Zones
S/S 1995

Patent Bow Mule

Les Femmes
S/S 1996

Stripe Sandal

Les Femmes
S/S 1996

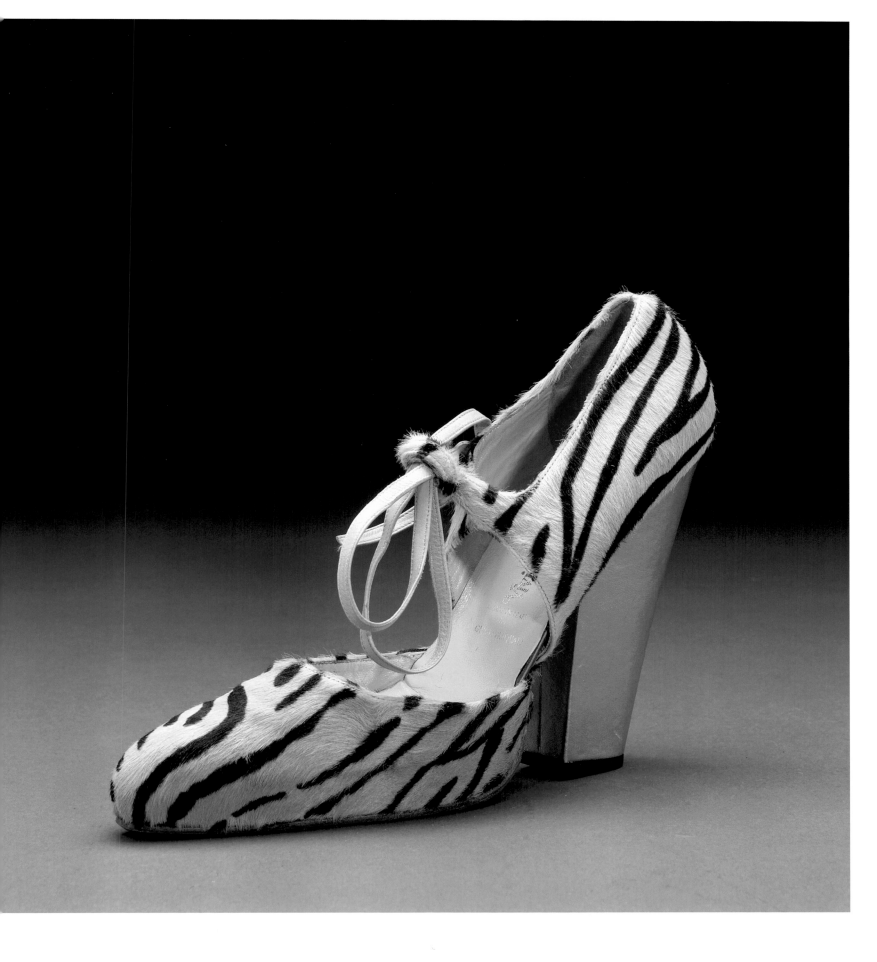

p 76

Toile Print Boot

Les Femmes
S/S 1996

Satyr Sandals with Ankle Tie

Vive la Cocotte
A/W 1995

Satyr d'Orsay Pump

Vive la Cocotte
A/W 1995

Tiger Satyr Ankle Boot

Vive la Cocotte
A/W 1995

Black Satyr Court

Vive la Cocotte
A/W 1995

Black Trompe l'Oeil Boot

Vive la Cocotte
A/W 1995

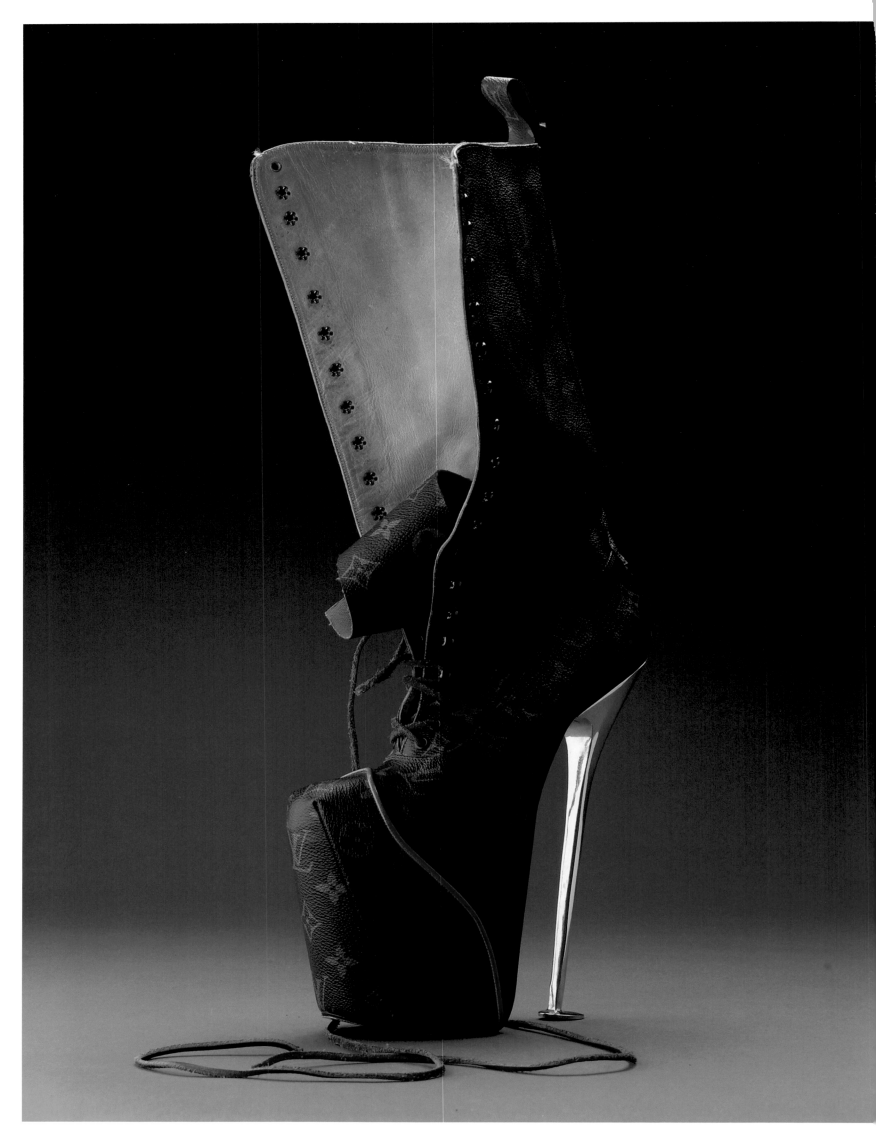

Trompe l'Oeil Tie Court

Storm in a Teacup
A/W '96

Trompe l'Oeil Court

Storm in a Teacup
A/W '96

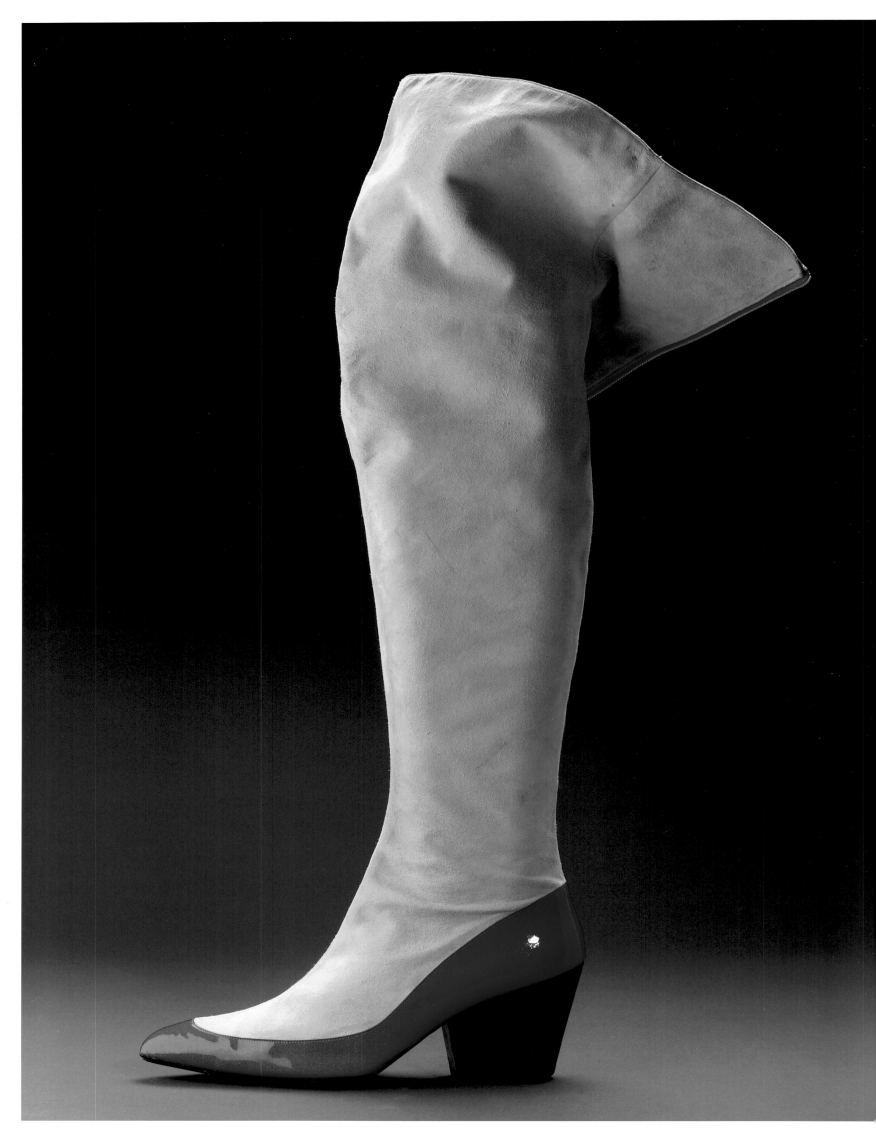

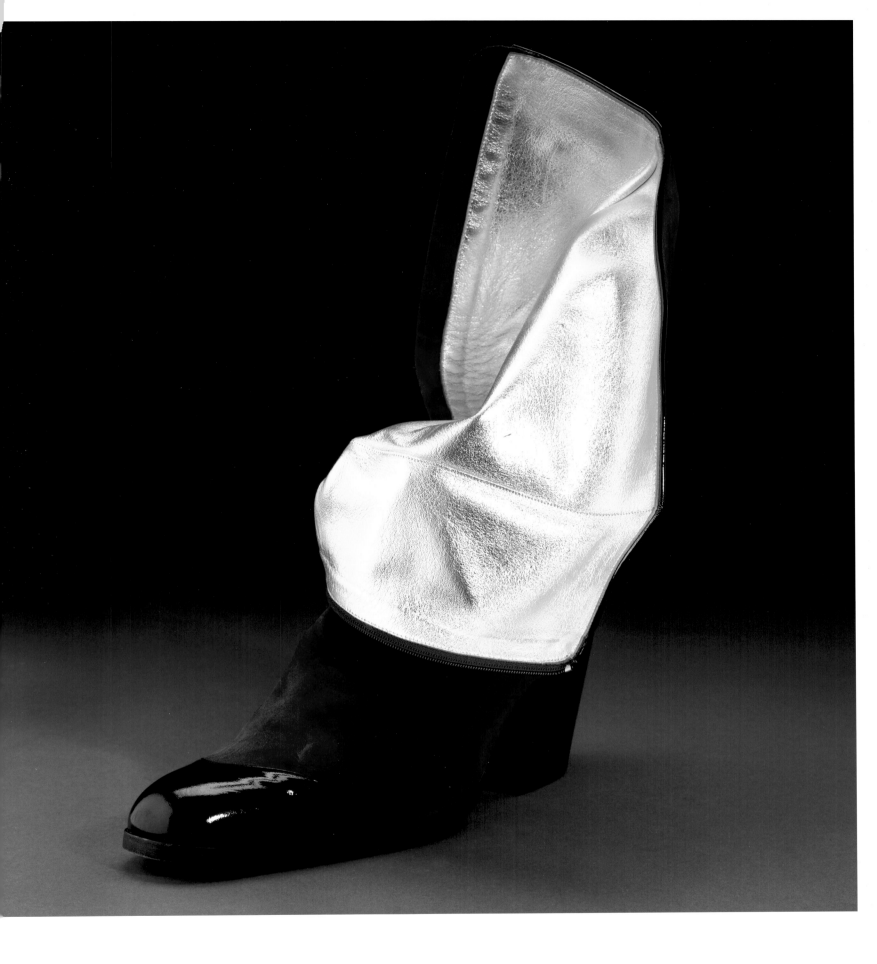

p 88

Trompe l'Oeil Boot

Storm in a Teacup
A/W 1996

Trompe l'Oeil Boot

Man
A/W 1996

Patent Slipper

Man
A/W 1996

Two Tone Gillie

Man
A/W 1996

Tudor Boot

Man
A/W 1998

Fringed Loafer

Man
S/S 1997

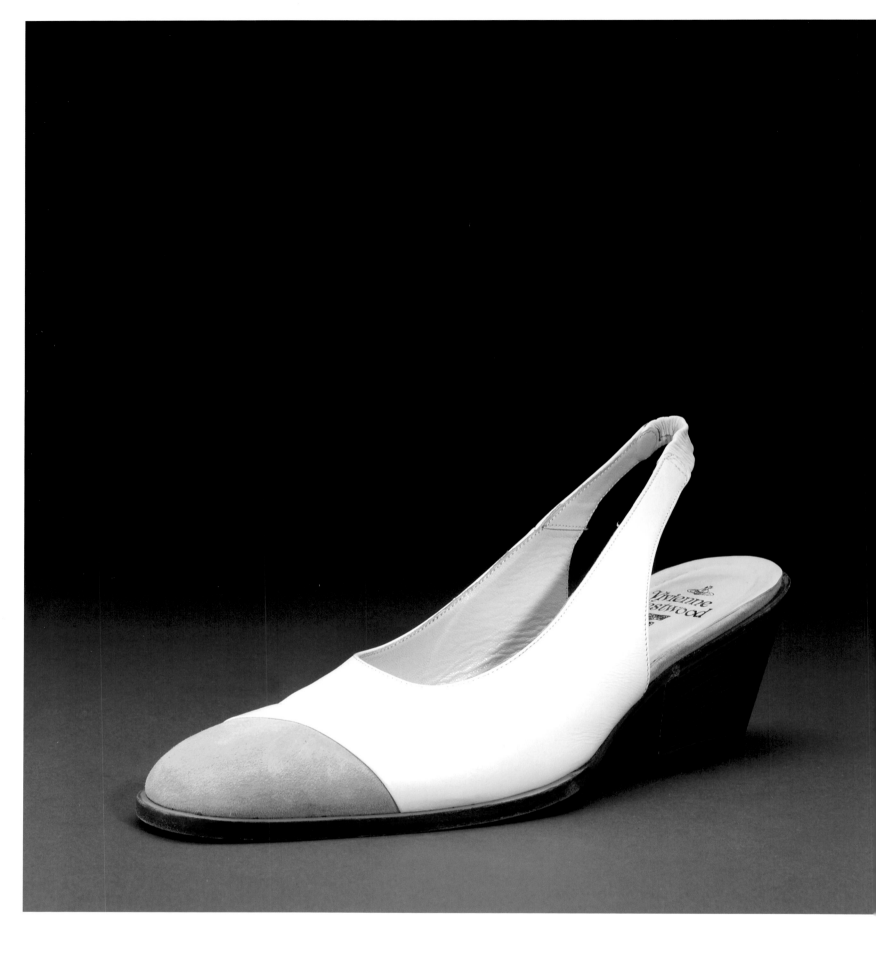

Two-Tone Sling Back

Man
S/S 1997

Metallic Shoe

Man
S/S 1997

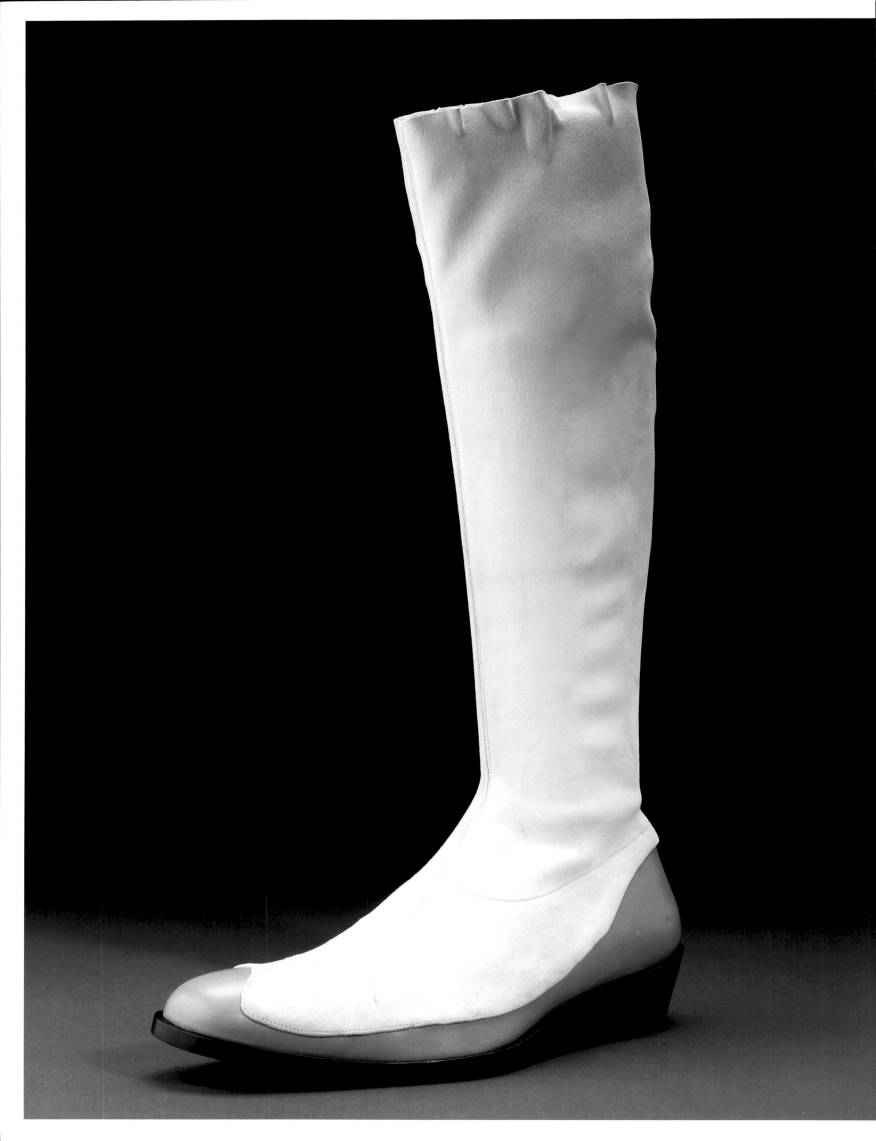

p 96

Circo Boot

Man
A/W 1998

Circo Slipper

Man
A/W 1998

Leather Three Strap

Man
A/W 1998

Sahara Plimsoll | Sahara Boot

Man
S/S 1999

Flame Shoe

Tied to the Mast
S/S 1998

Candy Stripe Gillie

Tied to the Mast
S/S 1998

Linen Pirate Boot

Tied to the Mast
S/S 1998

Elevated Ankle Boot

Dressed to Scale
A/W 1998

Two-Tone Charlie Shoe

La Belle Helene
S/S 1999

Two-Tone Court

Winter
A/W 2000

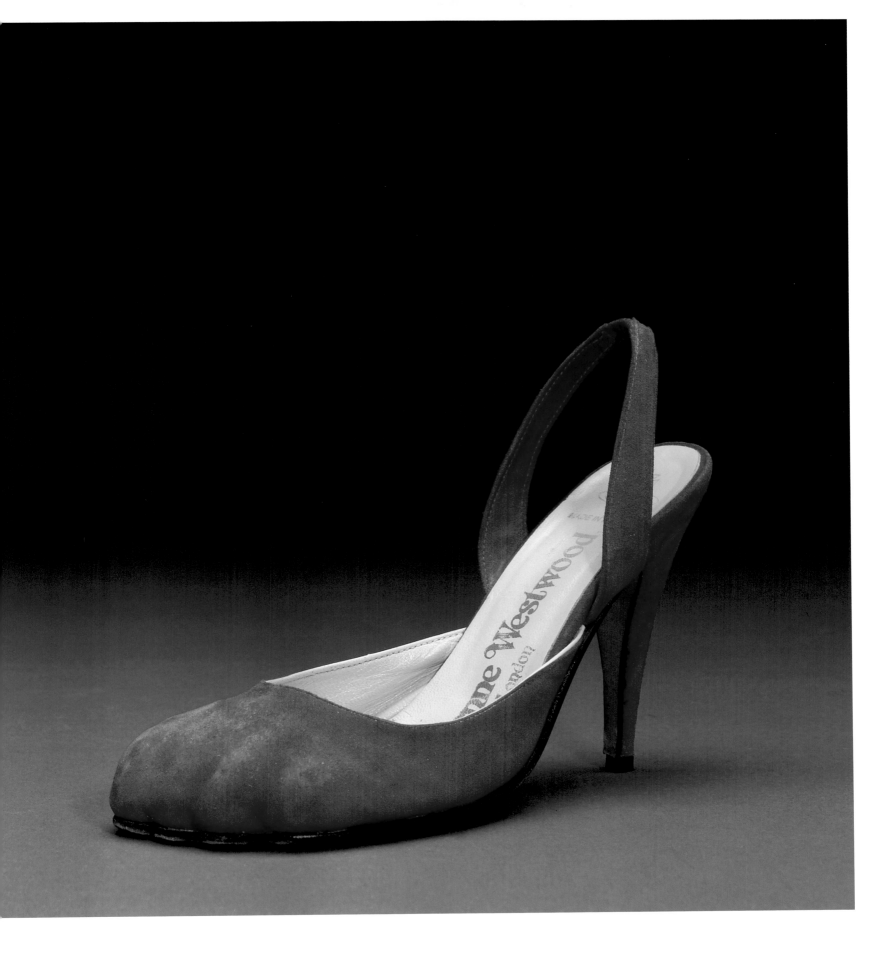

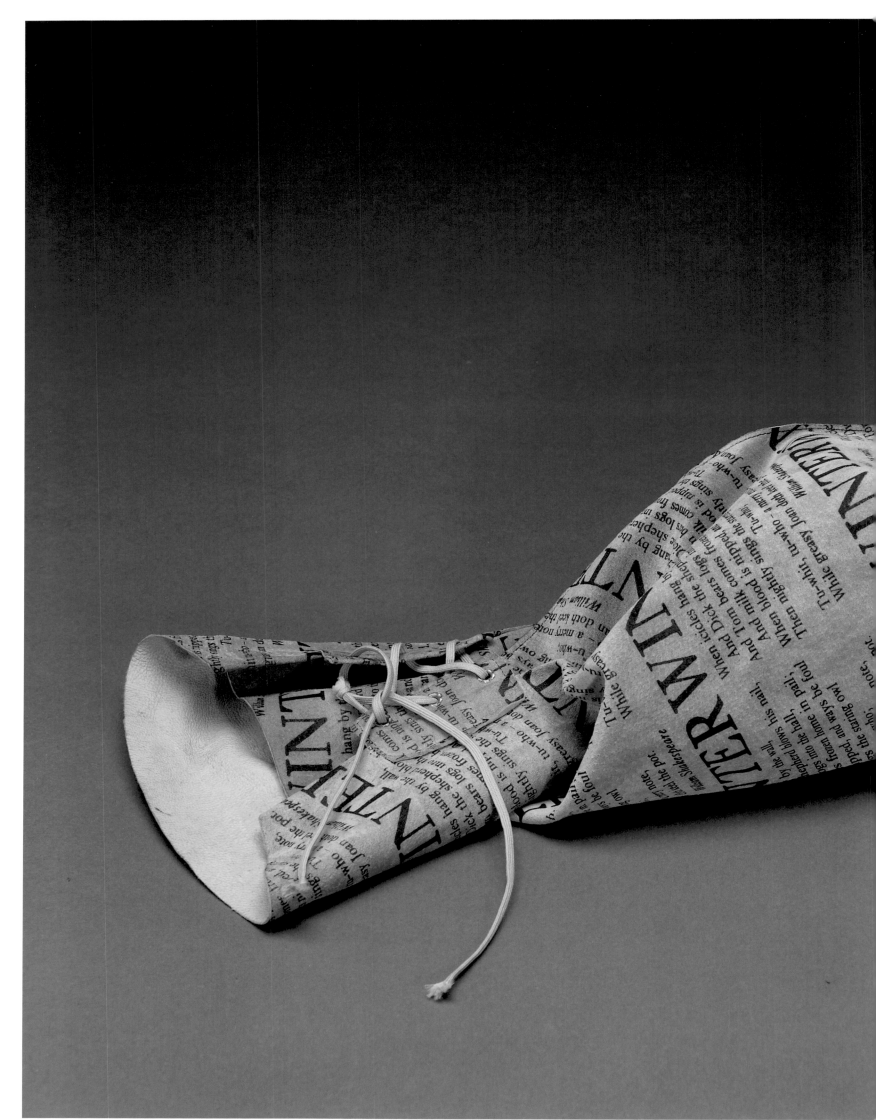

Green Satin Winter Boot

Winter
A/W 2000

Winter Newsprint Boot

Winter
A/W 2000

Brocade Mule

Summertime
S/S 2000

Exploration Brocade Gillie

Exploration
S/S 2001

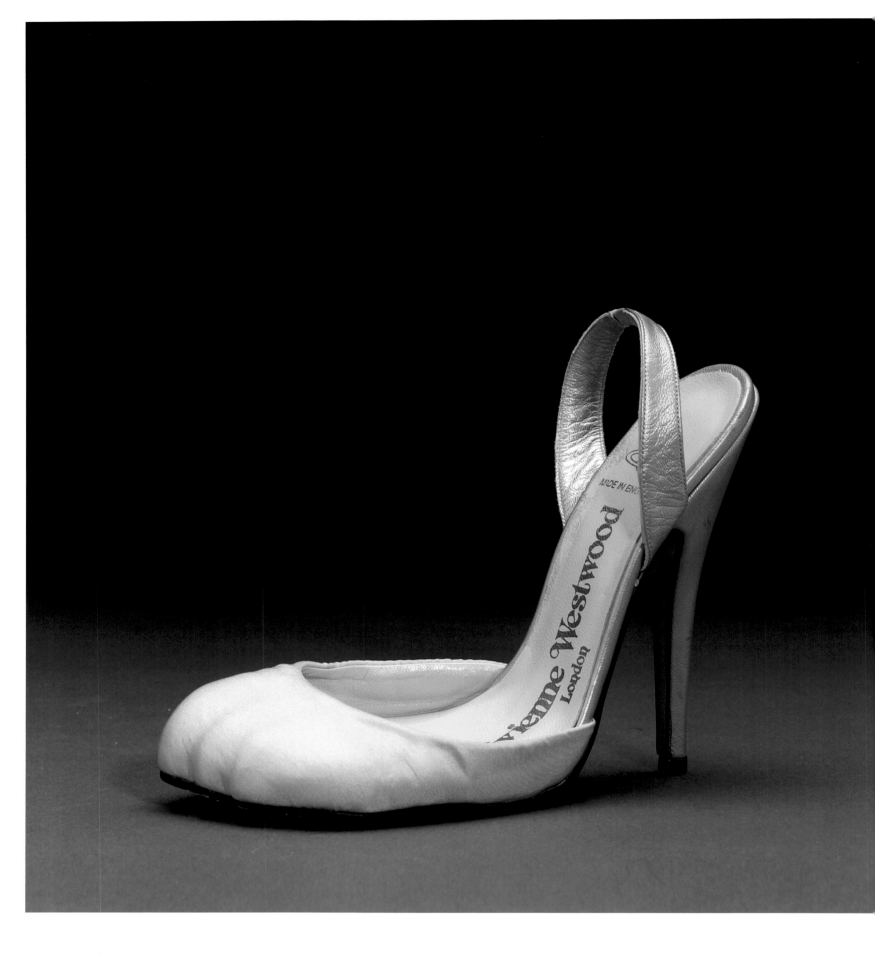

Exploration Sling Back

Exploration
S/S 2001

Three Strap Toe Shoe

Nymphs
S/S 2002

Canvas Seditionary Boot

Nymphs
S/S 2002

Bell Sandal

Nymphs
S/S 2002

Antique Bootee

Le flou taillé
A/W 2003

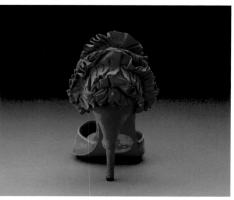

Auntie Maud

Le flou taillé
A/W 2003

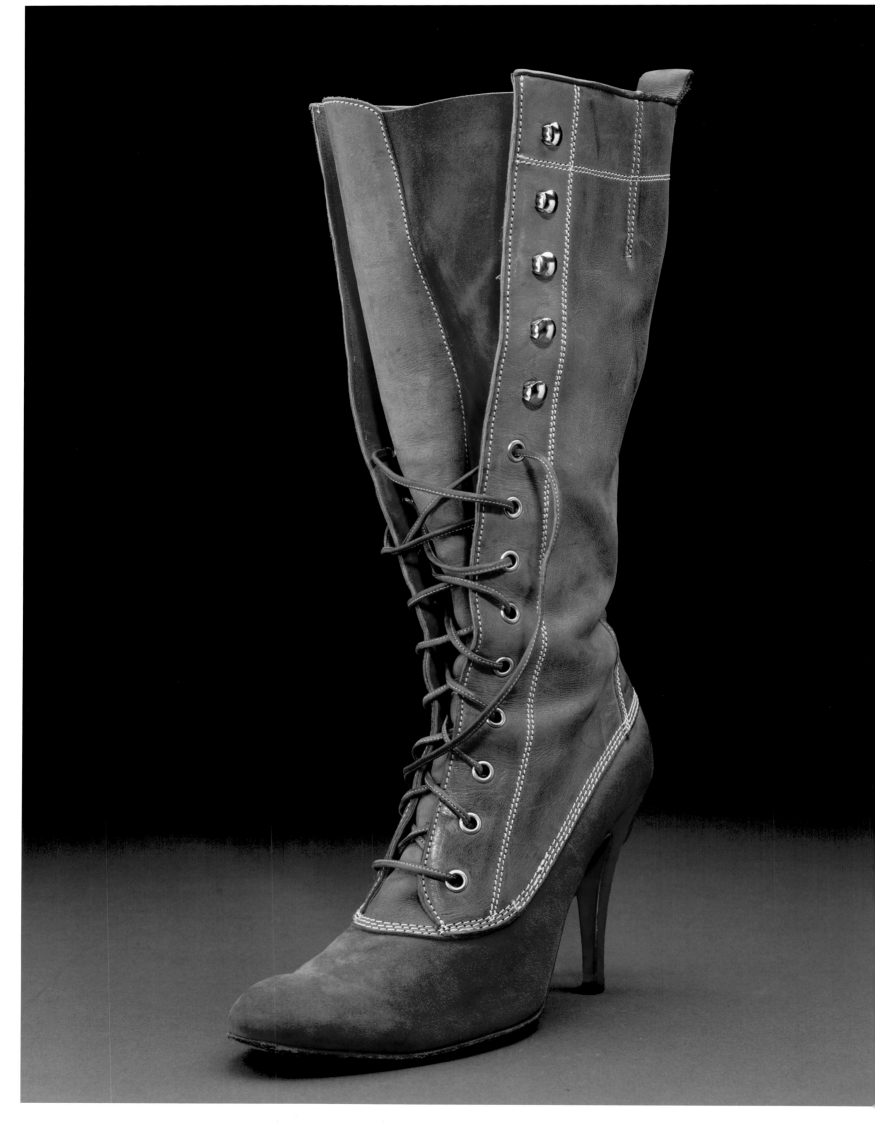

p 124

Duck Boot

Le flou taillé
A/W 2003

Jazz Shoe

Le flou taillé
A/W 2003

Tiger Print Sandal

Man
S/S 2004

Tiger Print Oxford

Man
S/S 2004

Flower

BLACK

WHITE dack

MAN'S BOX CALF OXFORDS!

STICHED like Berluti
SHOES

Caveman Sandals

Man
S/S 2004

Elvated Caveman

Blue Sky
S/S 2004

Petit-Pied Eyelet Lace-Up

Blue Sky
S/S 2004

Petit-Pied Fabric Sandal

Blue Sky
S/S 2004

Frilly Petit-Pied Sandal

Blue Sky
S/S 2004

Petit Pied Pompom Sandal

Blue Sky
S/S 2004

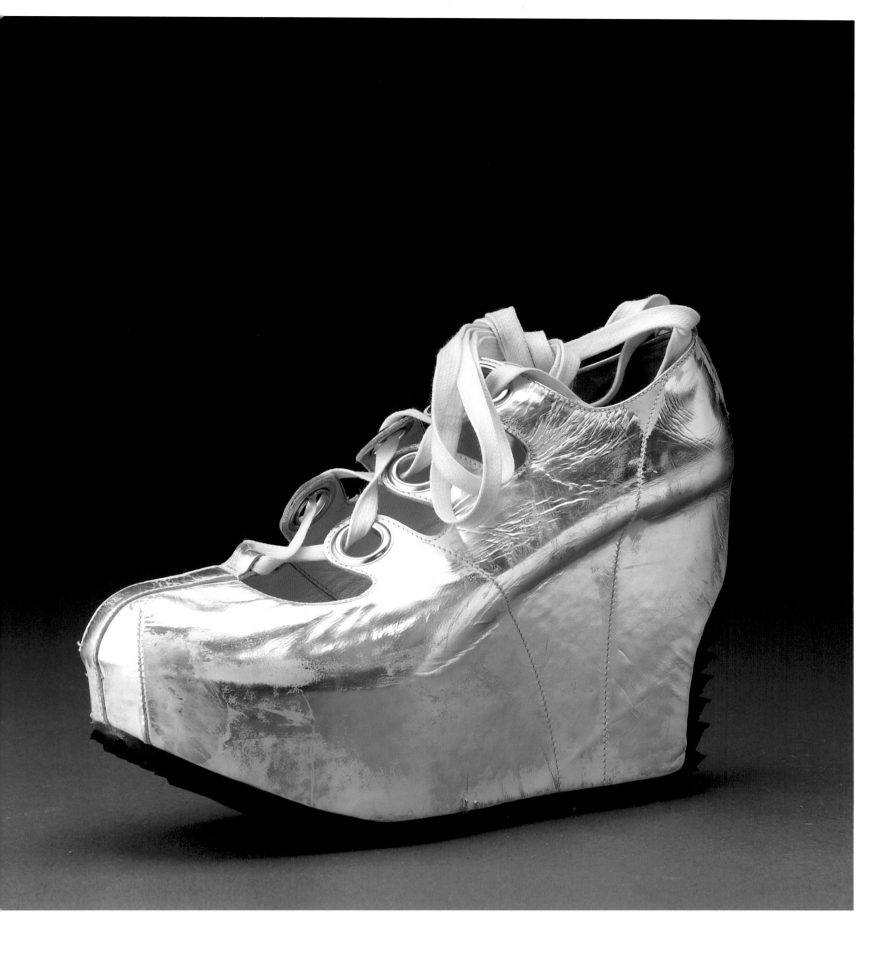

Silver Exhibition Gillie

Exhibition
A/W 2004

p 136

Exhibition Tight Boot

Exhibition
A/W 2004

Super Elevated Exhibition Shoe

Exhibition
A/W 2004

Bondage Sandal

Exhibition
A/W 2004

Can Shoes

Ultra Femininity
S/S 2005

Coin Sandals

Man
S/S 2005

Squiggle Granny

Ultra Femininity
S/S 2005

Ballerina Slipper

Ultra Femininity
S/S 2005

Propaganda Pirate Boots

Propaganda
A/W 2005

Propaganda Court

Propaganda
A/W 2005

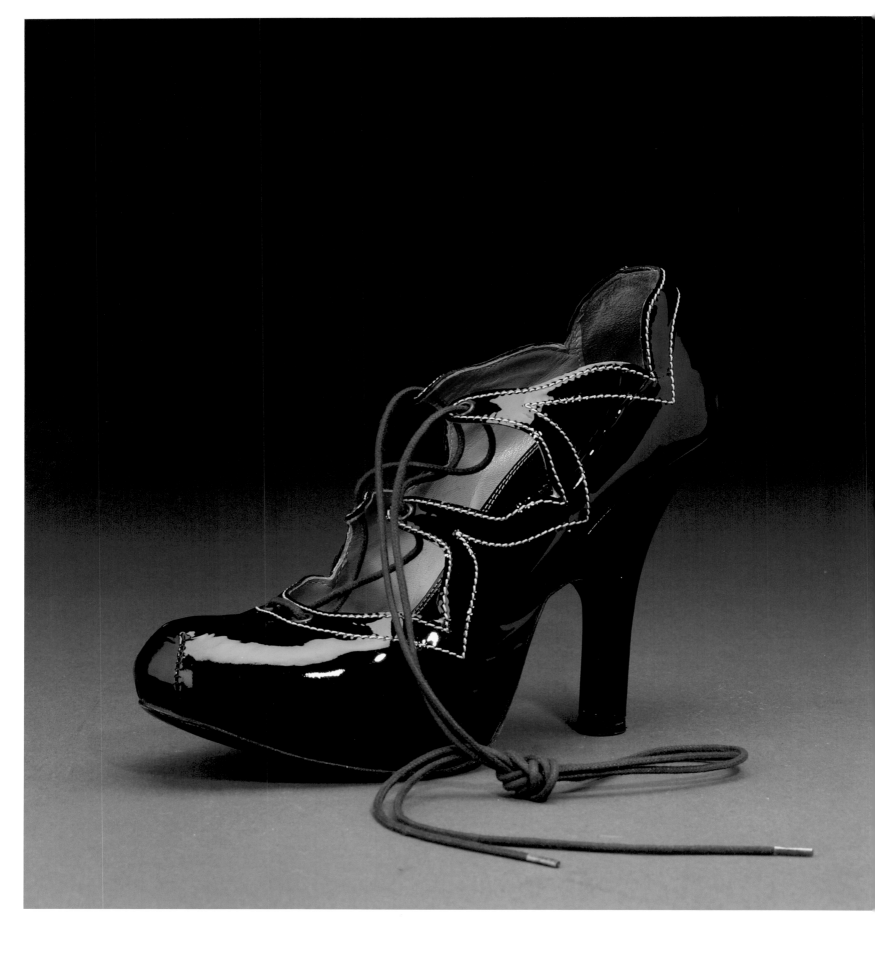

Propaganda Gillie

Propaganda
A/W 2005

Snake Shoe

Man
S/S 2005

Duck Shoe

Man
A/W 2005

Man Pirate Boot

Man
A/W 2005

AR Oxford

AR
S/S 2006

AR Mexican Sandal

AR
S/S 2006

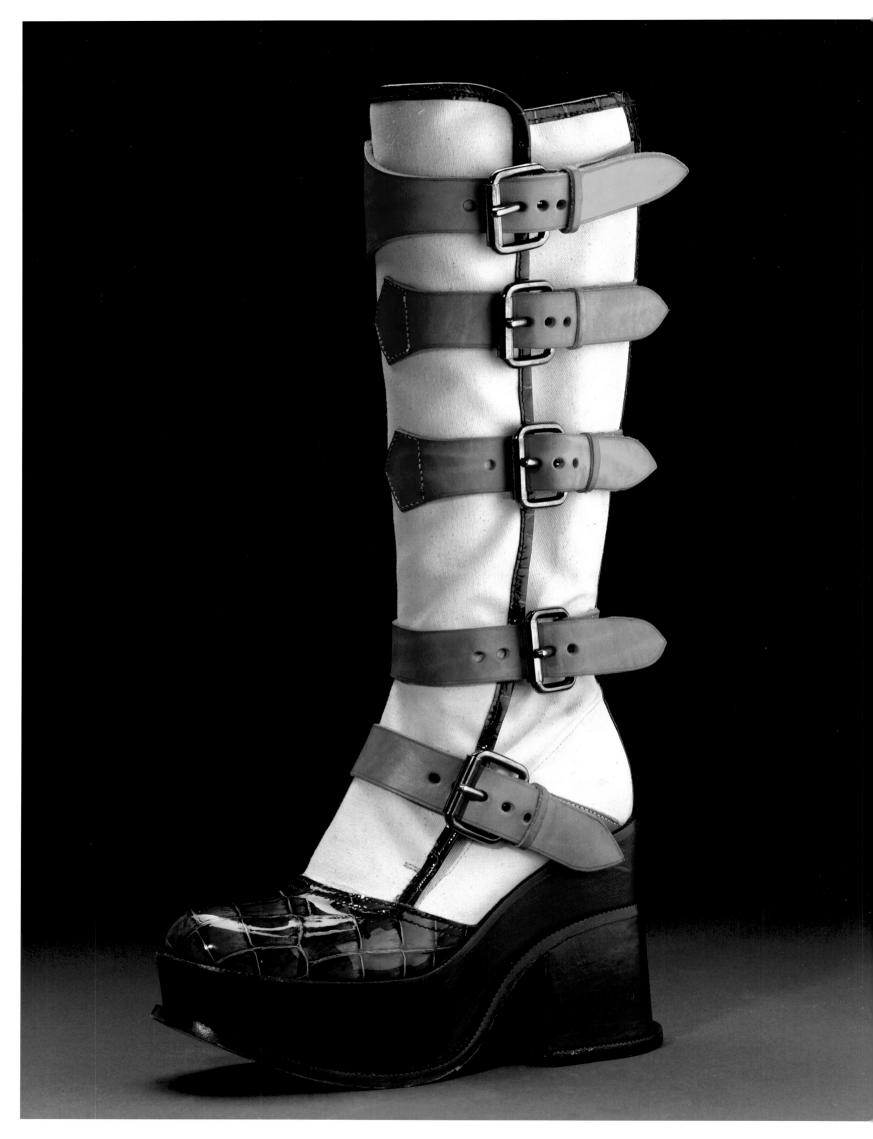

p 152

AR Pirate Boot

AR
S/S 2006

AR Elevated Bondage Boot

AR
A/W 2006

AR Three Tongue

AR
S/S 2006

Mirror Oxford

Man
A/W 2005

Teeth Shoe

Man
A/W 2005

Glitter Boot

Innocent
A/W 2006

p 158

Metallic Boot

Innocent
A/W 2006

Three Strap Prostitute

Innocent
A/W 2006

Fluo Oxford

Man
S/S 2007

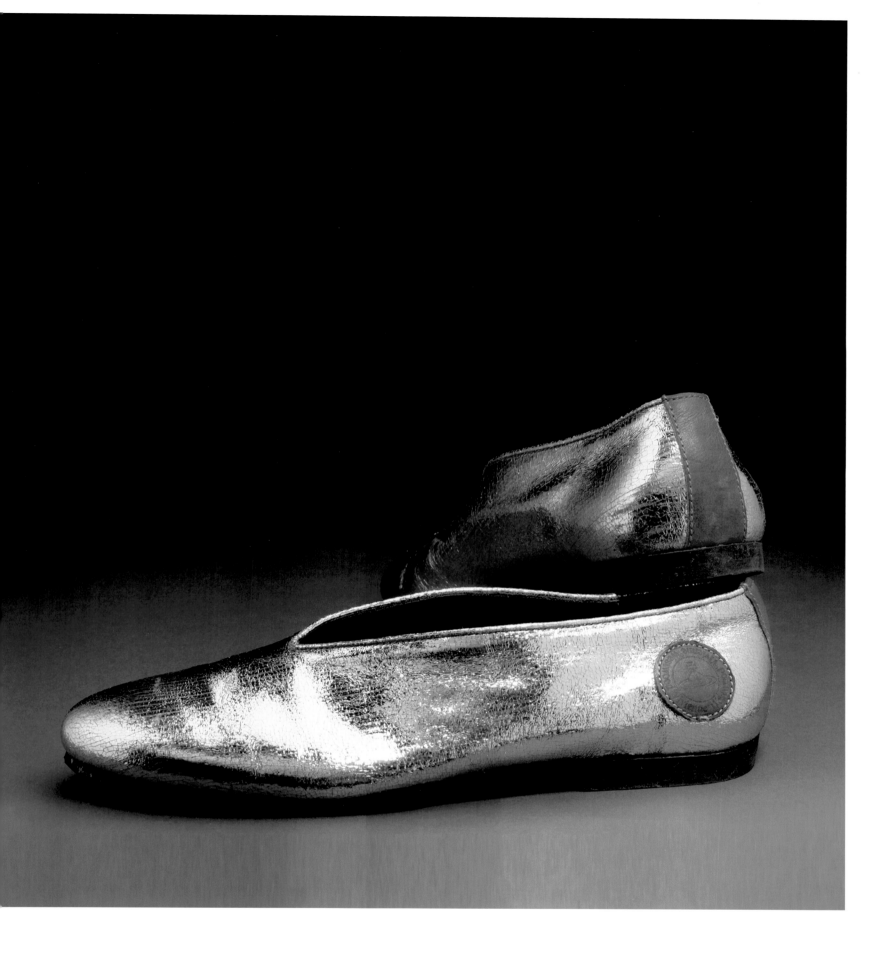

Gold Slipper

Man
S/S 2007

016|Vivienne Westwood's personal "Goat" Chain Boot
Sex 1973/74. Upper and leg in black fabric, toe and heel in black patent leather. Outside detail in wool. Wool lining. Leather insole.

017|Seditionary Boot
Seditionaries 1976. Upper in red leather with silver metal detail on the toe cap. Fastening at instep and ankle with metal buckles. Leather lining and insole. Leather sole.

018|Hammerhead Trainer
Pirate A/W 1981. Black leather shoe with red stripes and trim. Canvas lining, leather insole. Stacked heel in black leather. Leather sole.

019|Silver Hammerhead Boot
Savage S/S 1982. Upper in punched silver suede. squeare toe. Canvas lining and leather insole. Small brass bells attached on the back of the leg at anke level. Spool-shaped heel covered in silver leather. Leather sole.

020| *Honey* Magazine, 1982.

021|Brocade Hammerhead Ankle Boot
Savage S/S 1982. Multicoloured floral pattern brocade upper with mirror detail. Toecap in orange leather. Top part of the leg in orange leather, drawstring closure with leather lace. Canvas lining and leather insole. Spool-shaped hell covered in orange leather. Leather sole.

022|Rope Sandal
Punkature S/S 1983. Open sandal consisting of one piece matt white rubber unit with drawstring construction. Lilac cotton string and ankle fastening.

023|Rope Thong Sandals
Hypnos S/S 1984. Sandal, reference to the Japanese "zori", in matt-white rubber with lacing to the ankle/leg in lilac cotton string.

024|Witches Three Tongue Shoe
Witches A/W 1983. White leather upper with three large tongues. Fastened at the ankle with ribbons/strings in cotton. Leather lining and insole. White leather curtain detail covering heel.

025|Three Tongue Trainer
Witches A/W 1983. Trainer with high upper in white leather and three outsize tongues. Laces and oval eyelets in chrome. Leather lining and rubber insole. Rubber sole.

026|Strobe Shoe
Clint Eastwood A/W 1984. Upper in black patent leather with tongue resting on the topmost part of the shoe. Leather lining. Rubber sole.

027|Apollo Wing Shoe
Pagan I S/S 1988. Sandal with white leather upper. Looped straps and ankle fastening with a gilt "orb" logo button. Plastic wing decoration applied at the ankle. Monobloc rubber wedge, "profiled" and "inlaid".

028|Patent Mule
Pagan I S/S 1988. Upper in black patent leather with ankle strap. Low cut toe. Leather insole and lining. High heel covered in black patent leather. Leather sole.

029|White Boot with Mirror Eyelets
Voyage to Cythera A/W 1989. Upper in ivory patent leather. Boot fastened by satin ribbons laced through Plexiglas mirror worked rings. Leather lining and insole. High heel covered in ivory patent leather. Leather sole.

030| *Pirate Collection* A/W 1981.
Photograph by Robyn Beeche

031|Red Boot with Mirror Buckles
Voyage to Cythera A/W 1989. Upper and leg in red patent leather. Boot fastened by red patent leather strips closed by decoraive mirror worked Plexiglas buckles. Leather lining and insole. High heel covered in red patent leather. Leather sole.

033|Pirate Boots
Pirate A/W 1981. Boots in a variety of either suede or multicolored leather uppers. Fastening with metal buckles and natural leather straps. Leather insole. Stacked leather heel. Leather sole.

034|Pirate Slingback
Man S/S 2002. Men's casual sling back with upper in striped silk. Metal buckle fastening. Leather lining and insole. Stacked leather heel.

035|Pirate Ankle Boot
Man S/S 2002. Men's ankle boot with upper in beige suede and striped silk fabric. Fastening at instep and ankle with natural leather straps and metal buckles. Leather lining and insole. Stacked leather heel.

036|*Pirate Collection*, A/W 1981. Invitation to the first Vivienne Westwood and McLaren show. Photograph by Andy Earl.
Courtesy Vivienne Westwood.

037|Three Strap Sandal
Savage S/S 1982. Brown leather upper.Three straps detail and metal buckle fastening. Leather lining and insole, stacked leather heel. Leather sole.

038|Canvas Three Strap
Man S/S '02. Man's shoe with upper in ivory coloured canvas. Three strap detail eyelets and metal buckle fastening. Leather lining and insole. Stacked heel. Leather sole.

039|Buffalo Sack Boot
Buffalo A/W 1982. Low boot with upper in caramel leather. Leather lace closure at ankle. "Sack" effect on the instep. Leather lining and insole. Low cone leather heel. Leather sole.

040|Buffalo Bag Boot
Buffalo A/W 1982. One piece upper in pearl grey suede. Drawstring closure at ankle. Leather lining and insole. Cone heel covered in grey suede. Leather sole.

041|Anglophilia Sack Boot
Anglophilia A/W 2002. Boot with upper in brown leather and lacing around the ankle. Toe-cap in brown calfskin and special profiled working (toes). Leather lining and insole. Flared heel covered in leather. Leather sole.

042|Anglophilia Bag Boot
Anglophilia A/W 2002. Leg with one-piece upper in black leather. Drawstring fastening at ankle. Cotton laces. Stiletto heel covered in black leather. Leather sole.

043|Elevated Court
Portrait A/W 1990. Low cut shoe with biscuit coloured suede upper which extends to cover the platform. Leather lining and insole. 16 cm. heel covered in suede. Leather sole.

044|Elevated Tartan Lace-Up
Anglomania A/W 1993. Lace-up shoe with tartan upper. Toe-cap and heel counter in black patent leather. Leather lining and insole. 16 cm. heel covered in patent leather. Leather sole.

045|Elevated Court
Portrait A/W 1990. Low cut shoe with black patent leather upper in a single piece also covering the platform. Leather lining, sock and insole. 16 cm. heel covered in patent leather. Leather sole.

046|Super Elevated Fur Boot
On Liberty A/W 1994. Boot with upper in grey sheepskin. Upper extended to cover the platform. Leather lining and insole. Super elevated flared heel, 21cm in wood. Leather sole.

047|Elevated Wing Shoe
Portrait A/W 1990. Lace up shoe with brown leather upper. Calfskin wing shaped cuffs. Cotton laces in biscuit. Leather lining and insole. 16 cm. heel covered in leather. Leather sole.

048|Elevated Leopard Boot
Portrait A/W 1990. Upper in leopard print suede pigskin extending to cover the platform. Leather lining and insole. 16 cm. heel covered with the same material and design. Leather sole

049|Rocking horse ankle boots
Pagan I S/S 1988. Upper in black kid leather with zip fastening.
Leather lining. Profiled wedge heel in monobloc light-coloured wood. Rubber sole.

050|Sarah Stockbridge wearing Rocking Horse Ballerina, 1986. Photograph by Declan Ryan.

051|Rocking Horse Ballerina
Harris Tweed A/W 1986. Ballet pump with upper and laces in white leather. Leather lining. Monobloc wooden wedge, "profiled" and "inlaid".

052|Rocking Horse Golf Shoe
Time Machine A/W 1988. White and red leather upper with fringe to conceal the eyelets. White stitching. Leather lining. Monobloc wooden wedge, "profiled" and "inlaid".

053|Rocking Horse Slave Sandals

Pagan V S/S 1990. Sandal upper in gold leather. Ankle strap fastening with gilded metal buckle. Profiled and inlaid wedge heel in monobloc light-coloured wood. Rubber sole.

054|Super Elevated Lace-Up Ankle Boot

Grand Hotel S/S 1993. Boot with lacing along instep and ankle. Denim upper printed with floral motifs. Leather insole and lining. Upper extends to cover the platform. "Super elevated" flared heel, 21 cm., covered in fabric. Leather sole.
Note – Boots worn by Vivienne Westwood for her portrait by Juergen Teller – see catalogue cover.

055|Mock-Croc Super Elevated Court Shoe

Grand Hotel S/S 1993. Low cut shoe with upper in green mock-crocodile leather, upper also covering the platform. Leather insole and lining. "Super elevated" flared heel, 21 cm., covered in the same leather as the upper. Leather sole.

056|Naomi Campbell falling down during the *Anglomania* show (A/W '93), Parigi. Photo by Niall McInerney.

057|Mock-Croc Super Elevated Gillie

Anglomania A/W 1993.Upper in blue mock-crocodile leather also covering the platform. Traditional gillie construction with ribbon fastening. Leather insole and lining. "Super elevated" flared heel, 21 cm., covered in the same leather as the upper. Leather sole.

058|Cork Wedge

Cafè Society S/S 1994. Leather upper in nude colour extending to cover wedge. Leather lining. Wedge in leather covered cork. Rubber sole.

060|Beach Sandal on Cork Wedge

Cafè Society S/S 1994. Sandal with red leather straps crossed at the instep. White stitching. Leather lining. Monobloc cork wedge, "profiled" and "inlaid". Rubber sole.

061|Candystripe Fabric Tie Sandal

Cafè Society S/S 1994. Upper in red and white candy stripe cotton with fastening at ankle. Fabric lining. Monobloc cork wedge cut at the heel and profiled at the toe. Rubber sole.

062|Super Elevated Cowboy Boot

Cafè Society S/S 1994. Reworking of the cowboy boot. Leg in black patent leather with trim in silver leather.
Gold spray decoration on the front. Upper in black PVC with white floral motif that also covers the platform. Leather lining and insole. 19 cm stacked heel in wood. Leather sole.

063|Raffia Mule

Cafè Society S/S 1994. Lilac leather upper also covering the whole wedge. Decorated with coloured raffia and cotton volants on the topmost part of the toecap. Strass application on upper and wedge. Leather lining. Covered cork wedge.

064|Original illustrations by Vivienne Westwood

065|On Liberty Riding Boot

On Liberty A/W 1994. Upper and leg in black kid leather. Square toe. Brown leather band at the top of the leg.
Leather lining and insole. Stiletto heel covered in red leather. Leather sole.

066|Spanish Boot

On Liberty A/W 1994. Upper and leg in decorative fabric. Leather lining and insole. Stiletto heel covered in patent leather. Leather sole.

067|On Liberty C17ᵗʰ Shoe

On Liberty A/W 1994. Upper, toecap and tongue made in one piece purple leather. Red trim. Shoes fastened with a red leather lace. Reference to XVII century shoes. Stiletto heel 15.5 cm covered in white leather.

068|Mary Jane with Heart Buckle

On Liberty A/W 1994. Low cut "Mary Jane" model shoe in lilac leather. Strap at the instep with gilded, heart shaped metal buckle. Leather lining and insole. Stiletto heel covered in leather.

069|Lace Up Nurse Spoon

Erotic Zones S/S 1995. Nurse style lace up shoe with upper in kidskin white leather which extends to cover the platform. Leather lining and insole.Stiletto heel covered in white leather. Leather sole.

070|Two-Tone Court

Erotic Zones S/S 1995. Low cut shoe with white leather upper and black leather toe-cap. Punched details. Leather lining and insole.

071|Mary Jane Spoon

Erotic Zones S/S 1995. "Mary Jane" shoe with two-tone black and white upper. White leather strap with a gold orb gem button closure, the logo of the maison. Leather lining and insole. Stiletto heel covered in black leather. Leather sole.

073|Penis Shoe

Erotic Zones S/S 1995. Sling back with black suede upper and penis shaped decoration in synthetic material on the toe-cap. Strap and buckle fastening at instep. Leather lining and insole. Stiletto heel covered in suede. Leather sole.

074|Patent Bow Mule

Les Femmes S/S 1996. Low cut mule with white patent leather upper and bow in grosgrain. Leather insole and lining. Cone stacked heel. Leather sole.

075|Stripe Sandal

Les Femmes S/S 1996 Sandal with blue and white stripe design PVC upper, strap and buckle fastening. Leather insole and lining. Black cone stacked heel. Leather sole.

076|Toile Print Boot

Les Femmes S/S 1996. Upper in white PVC with Blue Toile print. Leather insole and lining. Raised toe. Black cone stacked heel. Leather sole.

077|Satyr Sandal with Ankle Tie

Vive la Cocotte A/W 1995. Sandal with upper in leopard print horsehide, fastened with ankle tie. Leather lining and insole. Cuban heel, 14, 5 cm, covered in laminated gold leather. Leather sole.

078|Satyr d'Orsay Pump

Vive la Cocotte A/W 1995. Upper in gold leather. Toe-cap extended to cover the "petit plateau". Leather lining and insole. Cuban heel 14, 5 cm covered in laminated gold leather. Leather sole.

079|Tiger Satyr Ankle Boot

Vive la Cocotte A/W 1995. Upper in tiger print horsehide. Wing shaped cuffs. Red leather trim. Leather lining and insole. Cuban heel 14, 5 cm covered in laminated gold leather. Leather sole.

080|Black Satyr Court

Vive la Cocotte A/W 1995. Upper and leg in red silk. Upper extends to cover the "petit plateau". Cuban stacked heel 14,5 cm in wood. Leather sole.

081|Black Trompe l'Oeil Boot

Vive la Cocotte A/W 1995. Upper and leg in black suede with applied toecap in black patent leather. Leather lining and insole. Cuban black stacked heel. Leather sole.

082|Red Satin Boot

Vive la Cocotte A/W 1995. Upper and leg in red silk; detail of the upper which extends in one piece to cover the "petit plateau". Cuban stacked heel 14, 5 cm. Leather sole.

083|Flame Boot

Vive la Cocotte A/W 1995. Upper in black suede calfskin with flame decoration in antique pink patent leather. Leather lining and insole. Cuban heel 14,5 cm. Leather sole.

084|LV Boot

Vive la Cocotte A/W 1995. Boot with upper and leg in Louis Vuitton signature fabric. This boot was part of a special collaboration between Vivienne Westwood and the French Maison. Leather laces. Leather lining. Gilded stiletto heel.

085|Purple Trompe l'Oeil Ankle Boot

Le flou taillé A/W 2003. Upper in violet suede with red leather strap closed at the front of the ankle with a metal buckle. Toe-cap in red patent leather. Red leather lining and leather insole. Black Cuban stackedheel.

086|Trompe l'Oeil Tie Court

Storm in a Teacup A/W 1996. Low cut shoe with red patent upper with stone suede inset. Cris-Cross fastening at the instep with a blue suede ribbon. Leather lining and insole. Cuban stacked heel, leather sole.

087|Trompe l'Oeil Court

Storm in a Teacup A/W 1996. Low cut shoe with two tone upper in red patent and stone suede. Detachable floral detail in electric blue suede. Leather lining and insole. Leather sole.

088|Trompe l'Oeil Boot

Storm in a Teacup A/W 1996. Thigh boot with upper in stone canvas and red patent leather. Zip fastening. Leather lining. Leather sole.

089|Tromp l'Oeil Boot

Man A/W 1996. Boot with upper and leg in brown suede and toe cap in black patent leather. Gilt leather lining. Cuban black stacked heel. Leather sole.

090|Patent Slipper

Man A/W 1996. Men's slipper with black patent leather upper. Leather lining. Cuban black stacked heel.

091|Two-Tone Gillie

Man A/W 1996. Black patent leather upper with punching and brown suede details. Leather lace with tassels. Leather lining. Cuban black stacked heel.

092|Tudor Boot

Man A/W 1998. Man's boot in black suede. Leather insole and lining. Cuban black stacked heel. Leather sole.

093|Fringed Loafer

Man S/S 1997. Loafer with printed pigskin upper in shades of pink. Decorative topstitching in white leather, fringe at toecap. Leather lining. Cuban stacked heel.

094|Two-Tone Sling Back

Man S/S 1997. Men's sling back in white leather with toe in antique pink suede. Leather lining. Cuban stacked heel. Leather sole.

095|Metallic Shoe

Man S/S 1997. Men's shoe with fuchsia laminated leather upper, strap across instep and fastening with a large metal buckle. Leather lining. Cuban stacked heel.

096|Circo Boot

Man A/W 1998. Men's boot with white suede upper and leg. Asymmetric toe-cap in biscuit coloured leather. Leather lining and insole. Low 4cm heel. Rubber sole and heel.

097|Circo Slipper

Man A/W 1998. Low cut men's dress slipper with two tone upper in striped white fabric and black crocodile print leather. Asymmetric toe-cap leather bound top line decorative white bow. Leather lining and insole. Low 4cm heel in leather.

098|Leather Three Strap

Man A/W 1998. Men's shoe with black leather upper. Fastening at ankle with a metal buckle. Multiple leather straps. Leather lining and insole. Low 4cm heel in leather.

099|Sahara Boot

Man S/S 1999. Men's ankle boot with upper in ivory canvas and biscuit suede stripes. Toe in biscuit suede. Lace fastening with metal eyelets. Leather lining and insole. Rubber sole.

Sahara Plimsoll

Man S/S 1999. Men's shoe with sporty striped motif. Upper in ivory canvas and biscuit suede. Stripes and toe in biscuit coloured suede. Five hole lace fastening. Leather lining and insole. Rubber sole.

100|Flame Shoe

Tied to the Mast S/S 1998. Low cut shoe with kidskin yellow leather upper. Gem application on the toecap with tiny beads and orange and yellow horsehair feature. Leather lining and insole. Louis heel covered in orange leather. Leather sole.

101|Swarowski Sandal

Tied to the Mast S/S 1998. Sandal with metallic leather upper and pointed toe. Laminated leather lining, leather insole. Louis heel covered in red and gold Swarovski crystals.

102|Candy Stripe Gillie

Tied to the Mast S/S 1998. Low cut tongue less shoe with gillie style lace fastening. Upper in pink and white candy stripe fabric. Leather lining and insole. Louis heel covered in fabric.

103|Linen Pirate Boot

Tied to the Mast S/S 1998. Boot with upper and leg in grey linen. Frayed edges a feature. Red leather straps fastened at ankle and leg with silver plated buckles and decorative loops. Louis heel covered in red leather. Leather sole.

104|Elevated Ankle Boot

Dressed to Scale A/W 1998. Upper in brown leather with raw cut edges. White stitching. Lace fastening in yellow cotton. Fabric label on the upper part of the tongue. Leather lining. Stiletto heel covered in leather.

105|Two-Tone Charlie Shoe

La Belle Helene S/S 1999. Lace up shoe with two tone upper in leather and patent. Round toe with black patent toe cap. Leather lining and insole. Leather and rubber sole. Low round heel.

106 | Two-Tone Court

Winter A/W 2000. Two-tone low cut shoe with upper in cream suede. Special profiled working (toes) of the toe-cap in black calfskin. Leather lining and insole. Stiletto heel covered in ivory suede. Leather sole.

107|Red Summertime Sling-Back

Summertime S/S 2000. Low cut sling-back with red suede upper. Special profiled working (toe-shapes) of the toecap. Leather lining. Stiletto heel covered in red suede. Leather sole.

108|Green Satin Winter Boot

Winter A/W 2000. Boot with upper and leg in green raw cut silk. Toe cap in brown calfskin with special profiled working (toe). Fastening with laces beneath the knee. Stacked stiletto heel. Leather sole.

109|Winter Newsprint Boot

Winter A/W 2000. Upper and leg in suede featuring black newsprint. String lace closure at back of leg. Leather insole and lining. Stiletto heel covered in printed suede. Leather sole.

112|Brocade Mule

Summertime S/S 2000. Mule with brocade fabric upper. Leather lining and insole. Stiletto heel covered in same material as upper.

113|Exploration Brocade Gillie

Exploration S/S 2001. Tongue less low cut shoe with gillie style lace fastening. Red paisley brocade. Heel counter in green leather. Leather lining and insole. Stiletto heel 14cm in leather.

114|Exploration Sling Back

Exploration S/S 2001. Low cut sling back sandal upper in pink silk. Ankle strap in silver leather pearlised. Special profiled working (toe) Leather lining and insole. Stiletto heel 14cm covered in silver pearlised leather. Leather sole.

115|Exploration Three Tongue

Exploration S/S 2001. Upper and three raw cut tongues in silver laminated leather. (dark brown on reverse) Gillie style lace fastening with brown laces. Leather lining and insole. Stiletto heel covered in silver leather. Leather sole.

116|Three Strap Toe Shoe

Nymphs S/S 2002. Low cut shoe with canvas upper, printed with floral motifs. Three straps with buckle fastening. Leather lining and insole. Flared heel covered in printed canvas.

117|Nymphs Seditionary Boot

Nymphs S/S 2002. Upper in leather and fabric printed with floral motifs. Metal buckle and strap at the instep and ankle. Concealed lacing. Special profiled working (toes) of the toe-cap in black calfskin. Leather lining and insole. Flared heel covered in leather. Leather sole.

118|Let it rock outfit.
1971.

119|Canvas Seditionary Boot

Nymphs S/S 2002. Boot with upper in black leather and red canvas. Fastened with metal buckles at the instep and ankle. Leather straps. Special profiled working (toes) of the toe-cap in black calfskin. Canvas lining and leather insole. Flared heel covered in leather. Leather sole.

120|Bell Sandal

Nymphs S/S 2002. Sandal with suede upper and studed details. Coloured bells and decorative horsehair attached to the upper. Lining and insole in silver leather. 10.5 cm stiletto heel covered in black suede.

121|Antique Bootee

Le flou taillé A/W 2003. Low cut ankle boot with upper in cyclamen suede. Lace fastening with suede laces in cyclamen. Stiletto heel 10 cm covered in cyclamen.

122|Auntie Maud

Le flou taillé A/W 2003. Peep-toe sandal with brown leather upper and cyclamen suede ruffle detail. Topstitching detail. Ankle fastening with suede lace. Stiletto heel 10 cm covered in cyclamen.

123|Biba Shoe

Le flou taillé A/W 2003. Lace up shoe with cyclamen suede and brown upper. Tie closure at the ankle with suede laces. Leather lining. Stiletto heel 10 cm covered in cyclamen.

124|Duck Boot

Le flou taillé A/W 2003. Boot with cyclamen suede upper and brown leather leg. Lacing with eyelets and applied hooks. Decorative topstitching stitching. Lining in red and cyclamen leather. Stiletto heel 10 cm covered in cyclamen.

125|Jazz Shoe

Le flou taillé A/W 2003. Slip on shoe with upper in brown leather and cyclamen suede. Elasticated detail on vamp. Leather lining. Stiletto heel 10 cm covered in cyclamen. Leather sole.

126|Tiger Print Sandal

Man S/S 2004. Men's sandal with tiger print leather upper and multiple straps. Fastening at instep with metal buckle. Leather lining and insole. Stacked heel in leather.

127|Tiger Print Oxford

Man S/S 2004. Men's Oxford shoe with upper in perforated tiger print leather. Five hole lace fastening. Leather lining and insole. Stacked heel in leather.

128|Original illustrations by Vivienne Westwood

129|Caveman Sandals

Man S/S 2004. Men's sandal with leather upper in a selection of colours. Leather lining and insole. Low heel. Rubber sole.

130|Elevated Caveman

Blue Sky S/S 2004. Open toe sandal with suede upper, ankle fastening with suede laces and decorative tongue. Suede lining. 12 cm wedge heel covered in suede.

131|Petit-pied Eyelet Lace-Up

Blue Sky S/S 2004. Green canvas upper with frayed edges. Large eyelets and raw cut cotton laces. Canvas lining and leather insole. Fabric covered heel.

132|Petit-Pied Fabric Sandal

Blue Sky S/S 2004. Upper in ruffled fabric with metallic finish. Leather lining and insole. Heel covered in red leather.

133|Frilly Petit-Pied Sandal

Blue Sky S/S 2004. Upper in ruffled white suede on straps and heel counter. Leather lining and insole. Heel covered in red suede.

134|Petit Pied Pompom Sandal

Blue Sky S/S 2004. Open toe black sandal with raw cut leather pom-pom detail. Sock and straps in black suede. Lining in leather. Heel covered in black suede. Leather sole.

135|Silver Exhibition Gillie

Exhibition A/W 2004. Silver mirror leather upper with gillie style lace fastening. Leather lining. Monobloc wedge, "profiled" and "inlaid" in cork, covered in silver leather with rubber sole.

136|Exhibition Tight Boot

Exhibition A/W 2004. Thigh high boot with upper and leg in brown leather. Leather lining. Monobloc wedge, "profiled" and "inlaid" in cork, covered in leather with rubber sole.

137|Super Elevated Exhibition Shoe

Exhibition A/W 2004. Black leather upper with strap and metal buckle. Peep toe with cut outs on vamp. Leather lining. Heel covered in black leather.

138|Bondage Sandal

Exhibition A/W 2004. Two tone sandal with brown leather upper and vamp in black patent leather. High ankle strap with metal buckle closure. Metal ring detail. Leather lining. Insole in light coloured leather and black leather. Flared heel covered in black patent.

139|Can Shoes

Ultra Femininity S/S 2005. Leather upper with metal and grosgrain accessories. Ankle fastening. Platform and heel covered with printed tin. Leather insole. Leather sole.

140|Coin Sandals

Man S/S 2005. Men's thong sandals in different coloured suedes decorated with applied metal coins. Low heel in leather. Leather sole.

142|Squiggle Granny

Ultra Femininity S/S 2005. Lace up shoe with jacquard upper and leather trimming. Closure at instep with fabric laces. Fabric lining, leather insole. Stacked leather heel 7,5 cm. Leather sole.

143|Ballerina Slipper

Ultra Femininity S/S 2005. Ballerina slipper with dove-coloured suede upper and leather edging. Rubber sole unit. Black grosgrain bow detail at toe. Fabric lining and insole.

144|Propaganda Pirate Boots

Propaganda A/W 2005. Boot with upper and leg in biscuit colour suede. Fastening at instep, ankle and leg with brown calfskin straps and metal buckles. Leather lining and insole. Platform and 12 cm. heel covered in suede.

145|Propaganda Court

Propaganda A/W 2005. Low cut shoe with electric blue patent leather upper. Leather lining. Patent leather Louis heel 12 cm.

146|Propaganda Gillie

Propaganda A/W 2005. Low cut gillie style with cotton lace fastening. Upper in black patent leather with white topstitching. Leather insole and lining. Patent leather covered Louis heel 12 cm. Leather sole.

147|Snake Shoe

Man S/S 2005. Men's shoe with brown leather upper. Rubber toe and sole unit. Fastening at the instep with green laces. Leather lining and insole. Low heel in leather.

148|Duck Shoe

Man S/S 2005. Men's shoes with brown leather upper. Rubber sole unit with stitching at toe. Toecap edging with visible stitching in relief. Fastening at the instep with brown calfskin strap and metal buckle. Leather lining and insole. Rounded rubber sole.

149|Man Pirate Boot

Man A/W 2005. Men's lace up boot in jacquard fabric and natural leather trimming. Rubber toe and sole unit. Cotton laces. Canvas lining and insole.

150|AR Oxford

AR S/S 2006. Slip on shoe with canvas upper printed with bold typographical characters. Trim in brown leather. Canvas tongue. Leather lining. Stacked Louis heel 12 cm.

151|AR Mexican Sandal

AR S/S 2006. Sandal upper in printed canvas with leather heel counter. Leather lining and sock. Extra wide heel in plastic. Plastic wedge.

152|AR Pirate Boot

AR S/S 2006. Leather upper with leg in white canvas trimmed in brown leather. Fastening with leather straps and metal buckles at the leg and ankle. Leather lining. Extra wide heel in plastic. Plastic wedge.

153|AR Elevated Bondage Boot

AR A/W 2006. Boot in canvas and croc printed leather with twoleather straps at instep and ankle. Leather insole. Louis 12 cm stacked heel. Leather sole.

154|AR Three Tongue

AR S/S 2006. Canvas and leather upper with three tongues. Cotton laces and metal eyelets. Leather lining. Extra wide heel in plastic. Plastic wedge.

155|Mirror Oxford

Man A/W 2005. Men's lace up shoe in silver mirror leather upper. Decorative details in black calfskin. Fastening along the upper part of the foot with red laces. Leather lining and insole. Low stacked heel in leather.

156|Teeth Shoe

Man A/W 2005. Men's lace up shoe with printed leather upper. Five hole lace fastening. Leather lining and insole. Low heel in leather.

157|Glitter Boot

Innocent A/W 2006. Boot with upper and leg in silver glitter fabric. Leather lining. Louis heel 12 cm covered in the same material as upper. Leather sole.

158|Metallic Boot

Innocent A/W 2006. Upper and leg in metallic green leather. Leather lining and sock. Louis heel 12 cm covered in the same material as upper. Leather sole.

159|Three Strap Prostitute

Innocent A/W 2006. Metallic green leather upper with three straps, two at the instep and one at the ankle. Leather lining and sock. Louis heel 12 cm covered in the same material as upper. Leather sole.

160|Fluo Oxford

Man S/S 2007. Men's Oxford shoe in fluorescent orange leather upper. Three hole lace fastening at the instep. Leather lining and insole. Leather heel.

161|Gold Slipper

Man S/S 2007. Men's slipper with gold laminated leather and embossed leather stamp applied on side. Black strap in brown leather. Leather lining and insole. Rubber sole.

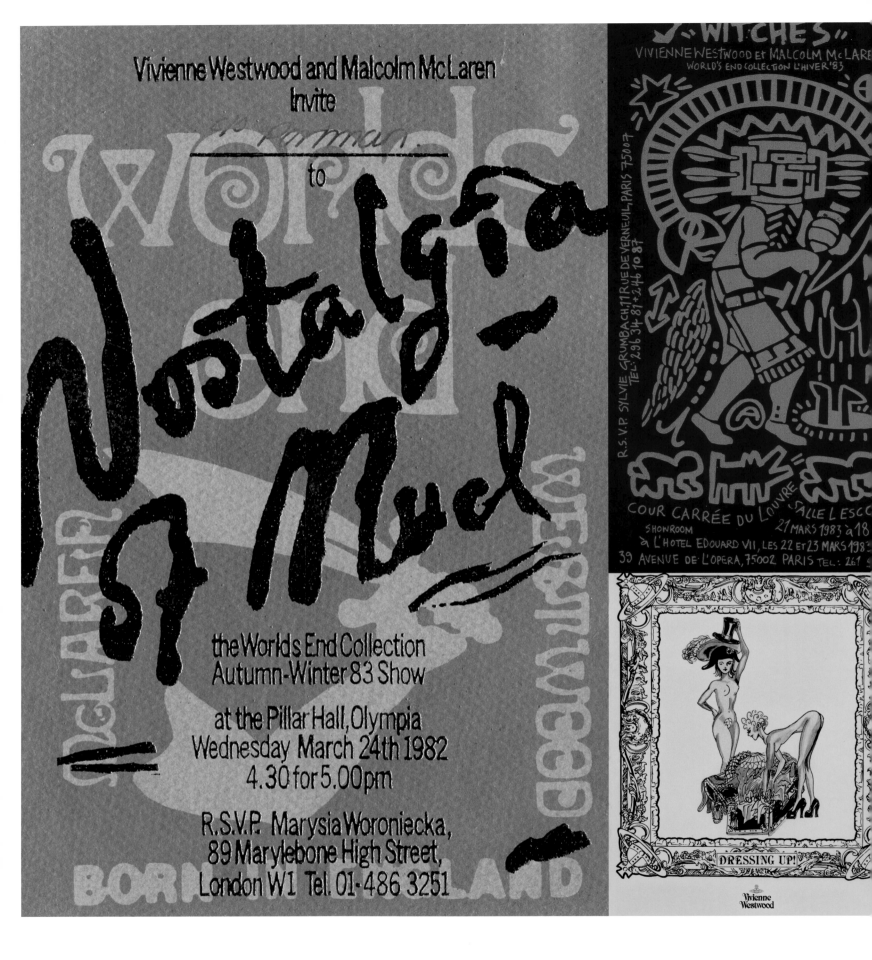

Vivienne Westwood and Malcolm McLaren
Invite
_____
to

Nostalgia
of Mud

the Worlds End Collection
Autumn-Winter 83 Show

at the Pillar Hall, Olympia
Wednesday March 24th 1982
4.30 for 5.00pm

R.S.V.P. Marysia Woroniecka,
89 Marylebone High Street,
London W1 Tel. 01-486 3251

"WITCHES"
VIVIENNE WESTWOOD et MALCOLM McLAREN
WORLD'S END COLLECTION L'HIVER '83

R.S.V.P. SYLVIE GRUMBACH, 11 RUE DE VERNEUIL, PARIS 75007
TEL: 296 34 81 + 246 10 87

COUR CARRÉE DU LOUVRE SALLE L'ESCO
SHOWROOM 21 MARS 1983 à 18
à L'HOTEL EDOUARD VII, LES 22 ET 23 MARS 198
39 AVENUE DE L'OPERA, 75002 PARIS TEL: 261 5

DRESSING UP!

Vivienne
Westwood

IENNE WESTWOOD AND MALCOLM MC LAREN S
SUMMER 1984

UR CARREE DU LOUVRE SALLE L ESCOT
MONDAY 17 OCTOBER 1983 AT 19 00 HRS
SYLVIE GRUMBACH 11 RUE DE VERNEUIL PARIS 75007
TEL 296 34 81 246 10 87
HOWROOM 4 RUE FAUBORG ST HONORE 75008 PARIS

VIVIENNE WESTWOOD
PRESENTS
CLINT EASTWOOD
WINTER 1984 COLLECTION
WORLDS END
SousA This
invitatioN is
VERY HorribLe

JARDIN DES TUILERIES SALLE PERRAULT
MONDAY 26 MARCH AT 19.00 HRS.
SHOWROOM: 4, RUE FAUBOURG ST. HONORE 75008 PARIS
TEL. 265 25 88

STORM
IN A
TEACUP

SALLᴱ SOUFFLOT
Lᴱ CARROUSEL ᴅᴜ LOUVRE
PARIS

FRIDAY 15ᵀᴴ MARCH
MCMXCVI
4.30ᴾᴹ

AUTUMN / WINTER
MCMXCVI / MCMXCVII

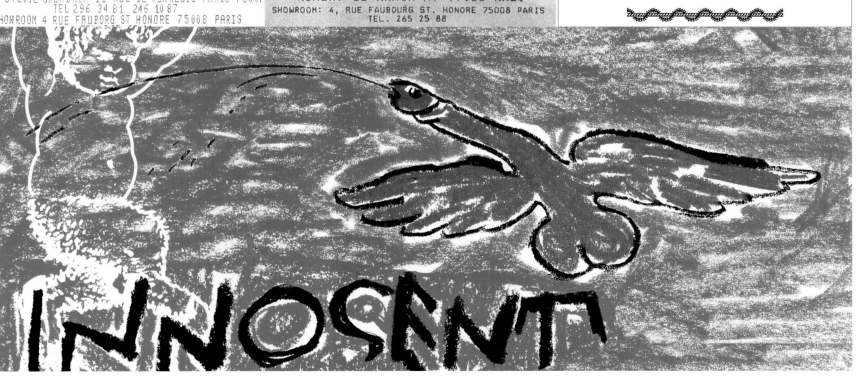

EXHIB

ITION*

APRIL 2004 - 11th OF JULY2004

172 | *Anarchy in the UK*
Extracts from the magazine published in
London, Mid 70's
Courtesy Vivienne Westwood

Jordan and Paul Getty shop assistant
outside the shop at 430 King's Road,
now called *Sex*, 1974. Courtesy Vivienne
Westwood

McLaren and Westwood launched punk
fashion and changed the shop's name to
Seditionaries, 1976.
Courtesy Vivienne Westwood

173 | Tracey wearing *Bondage* pants. 1975
Courtesy Vivienne Westwood

Toyah Wilcox wearing clothes from the
Seditionaries collection. 1976
Courtesy Vivienne Westwood

Vivienne Westwood and Malcom McLaren,
London, 1974. Courtesy Vivienne Westwood

174 | Tracey wearing *Blind Queen* T-shirt and
Bondage pants, 1976.
Courtesy Vivienne Westwood

175 | Toyah Wilcox wearing clothes from the
Seditionaries collection, 1976.
Courtesy Vivienne Westwood

176-179 | The artist Tracey Emin in the Vivienne
Westwood reportage in Paris, 2001.
Photo: Matt Collishaw
Courtesy Cosmic Galerie, Paris

180 | *Nostalgia of Mud*
Invitation to the presentation of the A/W
collection 1982/83, London.
Courtesy Vivienne Westwood

Witches
Invitation to the presentation of the
collection 1982/83, London.
Courtesy Vivienne Westwood

Dressing Up!
Invitation to the presentation of the
collection A/W 1991/92, Paris.
Courtesy Vivienne Westwood

181 | *Hypnos*
Invitation to the presentation of the
collection S/S 1984, Paris.
Courtesy Vivienne Westwood

Clint Eastwood
Invitation to the presentation of the
collection F/W 1984/85, Paris.
Courtesy Vivienne Westwood

Storm in a Tea Cup
Invitation to the presentation of the
collection A/W 1996, Paris.
Courtesy Vivienne Westwood

Innocent
Invitation to the presentation of the
collection *Gold Label,* A/W 2006.
Courtesy Vivienne Westwood

182 | *Exhibition*
Invitation to the presentation of the
collection *Gold Label,* A/W 2004, London.
Courtesy Vivienne Westwood

186 | Christian Shambenait, *Vivienne Westwood*,
2006.
Courtesy of the artist

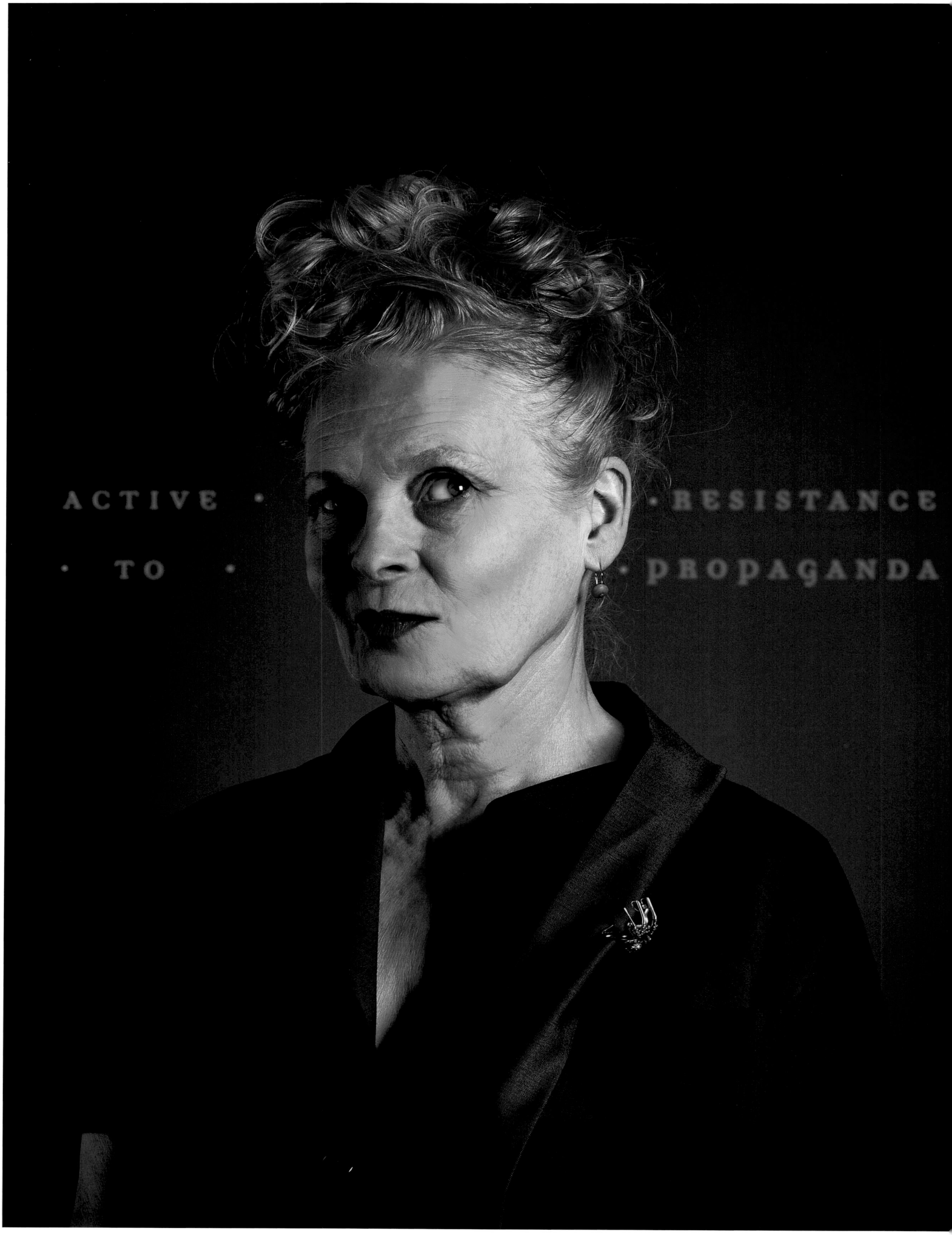
ACTIVE • • RESISTANCE
• TO • • PROPAGANDA

1941 | Vivienne Isabel Swire born 8th April in Glossop, Derbyshire

1957 | Moves with her family to London and attends Harrow Art School for one term.

1962 | At the age of 21 marries Derek Westwood and starts teaching at a primary school in Willesden, North London.

1963 | Her first child born, Benjamin Arthur Westwood.

1965 | Marriage with Westwood ends. Meets 18 year old Malcolm Edwards (aka McLaren).

1967 | She and McLaren have a son, Joseph Ferdinand Corré.

1971 | With McLaren she opens her first shop at 430 King's Road London called *Let It Rock*.

1972 | The shop is renovated and renamed *Too Fast To Live, Too Young To Die*.

1974 | The shop's name is changed again, this time to *Sex*.

1976 | N° 430 King's Road is renamed *Seditionaries*.

1979 | The shop's name is changed to its current one, *World's End*.

1981 | First show, *Pirate collection* (a/w 1981-82) presented at the Olympia, followed by the show *Savage* (s/s 1982).

1982 | *Buffalo* collection (a/w 1982-83) and *Punkature* (s/s 1983) presented in Paris. Westwood and McLaren open a second shop in London, *Nostalgia of Mud*.

1984 | Closes *Nostalgia of Mud* and moves to Italy.
Her relationship-collaboration with McLaren ends.
Invited to Tokyo for Global Fashion Awards, Hanae Mori's *Best of Five*, with the collection *Hypnos*, together with Calvin Klein, Claude Montana and Gianfranco Ferré.

1986 | Carlo D'Amario becomes Managing Director of the Vivienne Westwood company.

1987 | Designs the corset *Stature of Liberty* for the collection *Harris Tweed* (a/w 1987-88). The first corset intended as an outer garment rather than underwear.

1989 | Appears in John Fairchild's book *Chic Savages* (1989) as one of the world's six best fashion designers, together with Armani, Lagerfeld, Saint Laurent, Lacroix and Ungaro.
Awarded the title Professor of Fashion by the Vienna Academy of Applied Arts.

1990 | In December she opens the Vivienne Westwood monobrand shop, at 6 Davies Street In London's Mayfair, for sale of the Gold Label collection.
The British Fashion Council names her designer of the year.
In Florence with Pitti Uomo she shows her first complete menswear collection *Cut and Slash* (s/s 1991).
She is the first fashion designer to be featured in the arts programme *The South Bank Show* on London Weekend Television.
BBC Radio 4 broadcasts a special in which she interviews various figures from the world of artistic and cultural heritage preservation, this to underline that the stagnation of museums and art galleries is a direct result of government policies.

1991 | The British Fashion Council names her designer of the year for the second time and the Vienna Academy of Applied Arts confers her second title of *Professor of Fashion*.
Show at the Tokyo Fashion Summit with top designers Christian Lacroix, Isaac Mizrahi and Franco Moschino.

1992 | Made honorary member of the Royal College of Art.
Opens a shop at 43 Conduit Street, London.
Designs the *Putti* watch for Swatch.

Invited to present a retrospective at the Bordeaux Musée d'Art in France.
Buckingham Palace includes her in the Birthday Honours list. In December receives the O.B.E. from Queen Elisabeth.
Marries Andreas Kronthaler whom she met while teaching in Vienna.
In the spring/summer collection *Salon* Vivienne presents her first wedding dresses, made to measure. Unlike most other designers, she does not restrict herself to white and ivory.

1993| For the *Anglomania* collection she creates the *Mac Andreas* tartan in honour of her husband. It is recorded in the archives of Lochcarron museum for a process of recognition that generally takes 200 years.
Becomes *Professor of Fashion* at the Berliner Hochschule der Künste.
Designs her second watch, the *Orb*, for Swatch.

1994| In May she wins the *Institute of Contemporary Art Award for outstanding contribution to Contemporary Culture.*
Designs the *Ancien Régime* costumes in carpet to celebrate the 1783 founding of the carpet company Brintons.

1996| In January launches her menswear line *Man* in Milan.
In spring Channel 4 broadcasts the three part series *Painted Ladies.*

1998| Vivienne Westwood Ltd obtains the "Queen's Award for Export" in recognition of the company's growing exports.
Launches her first perfume Boudoir, developed with Martin Gras of Dragoco, internationally famous 'nose'. "My perfume is called *Boudoir.* The boudoir is a little room where you undress. This means that it's a wholly feminine place, a place where a woman enters into intimacy with herself, where she comes to terms with her faults and potentials."

1999| In February, tied in with the first Westwood shop opening in New York, she launches *Red Label* in the United States.

A line of accessories is introduced which includes *Eyewear and the Coquetteries Body and Bath Line.*

2000| The Museum of London hosts the exhibition *Vivienne Westwood: the collection of Romilly McAlpine* from 7th April to 25th June.
The second Westwood fragrance *Libertine* is launched in Europe.

2001| Official launch of website www.viviennewestwood.com.
The first fashion designer acknowledged at the "Moët & Chandon Fashion Tribute". This prestigious annual event pays tribute to the most authoritative exponents of the world of fashion whose creativity and vision of dress have deeply influenced our lifestyle.
Opens her first monobrand shop in Moscow (March).
On 8th April celebrates her sixtieth birthday: many leading figures of the northern European and International press pay homage, celebrating her brilliant career.
Libertine launched in the United States, the Middle East and Australia.

2002| Monobrand shop opens in Hong Kong.
Launch of two Westwood boutiques in Korea.

2003| Collaboration with Wedgwood. Two of the most famous and recognised English brand names meet to create a line for the home.
Receives the "UK Fashion Export Award for Design".
The Milan palazzo and boutique open in September. In October, a monobrand shop inaugurated in Liverpool.

2004| Obtains a "Lifetime Achievement Award" at the "Elle Style Awards".
In April the Victoria & Albert Museum in London holds a retrospective of Vivienne Westwood's 34 year career, the most extensive exhibition ever dedicated to a living English fashion designer.
Presented with the "Women's World Fashion Award" by former President Gorbachev in Hamburg.
Launches her third fragrance *Anglomania.*

2005| The collection of high quality jewellery *Hardcore Diamonds* is presented in Paris during the show *Gold Label* a/w 2005-06.

2006 | Granted the title of Dame in the "New Year Honours List".
In September at Castello di Vigevano, *Vivienne Westwood Shoes* opens, the first international retrospective dedicated to the English designer's shoe production.

VIVIENNE WESTWOOD SHOES

edited by
Luca Beatrice and Matteo Guarnaccia

SPECIAL THANKS
Vivienne Westwood, Andreas Kronthaler,
Carlo D'Amario.

ARTWORK
brh+
www.brh.it

SERVIZIO FOTOGRAFICO
Vivienne Westwood Ltd.

COVER
Juergen Teller, *Vivienne Westwood*, London, 1993.
Courtesy of the artist and Contemporary Fine Arts,
Berlin.

THANKS TO
Museo di Vigevano, Luca Beatrice,
Matteo Guarnaccia, Alex Krenn,
Margherita Protti, Margherita Remotti,
Giorgio Ravasio, Murray Blewett, Denise
Zamarioni, Ilaria Brustia, Valentina Cereda,
Hazel McDonald, Benjamin Shun Lai,
Beata De Campos, Joe De Campos,
Sara Pireddu, Studio Barbieri & Ridet.

DAMIANI©2006

Damiani Editore
Via Zanardi, 376
Tel. +39.051.6350805
Fax +39.051.6347188
40131 Bologna - Italy
www.damianieditore.it
info@damianieditore.it

Translation
David Smith

Printed on
Novatech Satin 170 gr
distributed by

© the authors for their texts
© the photographers for their photos

Printed in Italy
September 2006 by
Grafiche Damiani, Bologna